THE STATE OF THE ECONOMY

THE STATE
OF THE ECONOMY

Bill Martin · Giles Keating

Walter Eltis · David Lomax

Jonathan Haskel & John Kay

Gordon Pepper · Tim Congdon

Patrick Minford · Bill Robinson

Introduction by
Graham Mather

IEA
Institute of Economic Affairs
1990

First published in February 1990
by
THE INSTITUTE OF ECONOMIC AFFAIRS
2 Lord North Street, Westminster, London SW1P 3LB

IEA Readings 31

ISSN 0305-814X
ISBN 0-255 36230-7 (hard cover)
ISBN 0-255 36231-5 (paper)

The Institute gratefully acknowledges financial support for its publications programme and other work from a generous benefaction by the late Alec and Beryl Warren.

Printed in Great Britain by
Goron Pro-Print Co. Ltd., Lancing, W. Sussex

Filmset in 'Berthold' Times Roman 11 on 12 point

CONTENTS

Contents

INTRODUCTION

Graham Mather
General Director,
Institute of Economic Affairs

THE BRITISH ECONOMY stands at a paradoxical juncture. It saw real advances during the 1980s. They dramatically improved the supply side, transformed the performance of former nationalised industries, recast industrial relations and widened ownership. Tax rate reductions and privatisation became a model for economies across the OECD.

Yet by the end of the decade these achievements are overshadowed by the re-emergence of some traditional British economic problems. They go to the fundamentals of the Medium-Term Financial Strategy and pose serious questions as to whether there has, as yet, been established the stable framework of predictable policy which was intended to allow businessmen to plan and invest free from 'stop go' swings.

At the heart of this issue lies sound money. At the beginning of the 1990s it appears disturbingly clear that economists and policy-makers have still to achieve an effective system of monetary measurement and control, capable of functioning in deregulated financial markets without exchange control, and sufficiently robust to resist being overborne by policy misjudgements. During the late 1980s many economists appeared to have given up the search for this elusive system of monetary control. In 1990, as a number of papers in this book testify, the consequences of losing the way on the path to sound money and stable prices have lent a new vigour to the search.

The fundamental importance of a stable framework must head the economic agenda for Britain in the 1990s. The second, and no less difficult challenge, is to assess the macro- and micro-economic approaches which are conducive to strengthened competitive performance. This book focusses sharply on elements of Britain's performance, measured by the current account, by productivity, and in the labour market and the performance of education and training systems.

The picture revealed is mixed. It can be summarised very simply. The competitive advances achieved in the British economy during the 1980s have been profoundly significant and have demonstrably put Britain back on track as an enterprising, innovative and attractive location for investment. That said, it would be a profound mistake to confuse improved relative performance, and in particular the fast relative growth achieved during the late 1980s, with the levels of real output achieved by leading world economies. Measured by GDP output per capita, Britain's performance has lain around 16th in the OECD league table: still too far behind competitors in Europe, let alone North America and the Pacific Rim, for comfort. The legacy of 30 years of post-war competitive underperformance will clearly take more than a decade to cure, and it is now clear that this second challenge can be made doubly difficult if there is a wavering from the discipline needed to maintain a stable and predictable policy framework.

The 'catch-up' factor is addressed by a number of contributors to this book. Their suggestions are interesting and tend to be radical. In this, in the observations on productivity performance, and in monetary control, there emerges a surprising consistency of view: a suggestion that the British economy performs best when subject to shock, discontinuity, and radical reform.

The Institute of Economic Affairs is delighted to publish this book, with papers by a number of Britain's leading economists, as an important and informed contribution to economic education, understanding and debate. The views expressed in it are, of course, those of the authors themselves, not of the Institute or its Trustees, Directors or Advisers. I would like to extend thanks to them all for making possible such a useful and stimulating book.

February 1990

GRAHAM MATHER
General Director,
Institute of Economic Affairs

THE CURRENT ACCOUNT CONSTRAINT

Bill Martin
UBS Phillips & Drew

IT IS A TRUTH universally accepted that Mr Major was making it up. The story of hard times told in his Autumn Statement is roundly dismissed as a marketing ploy to boost the Chancellor's credibility as performer—though not as forecaster—when things turn out better. But the hard truth is that the Chancellor is an honest John. The sad fact about the state of the economy is that it is indeed in a state—thanks to the Lawson Legacy.

As every schoolboy knows, Mr Lawson arranged a modest pre-election expansion but then became addicted to growth. As a result he out-boomed Mr Barber. Chart 1 shows growth of onshore GDP—the GDP 'output estimate' excluding oil production. In 1987 and 1988, ex-oil growth was 5¼ per cent each year on official figures, which might well be revised up. In the first three-quarters of 1989 growth year-on-year was still 4 per cent. Although previous peak years have sometimes seen growth as high as 5-6 per cent, the near-11 per cent expansion of on-shore activity in 1987-88 is without precedent in the post-war period.

Behind this heady expansion lay a phenomenal private-sector-generated rise in domestic demand—the sum of consumption, investment and stockbuilding. In 1988, demand probably grew by 8-9 per cent and cumulatively by 14-15 per cent over the Lawson boom

Chart 1:   UK Growth Cycle

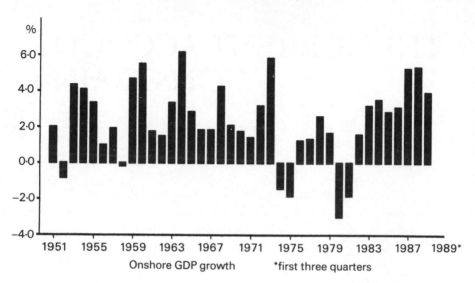

Onshore GDP growth   *first three quarters

Chart 2:   UK Domestic Demand Growth†

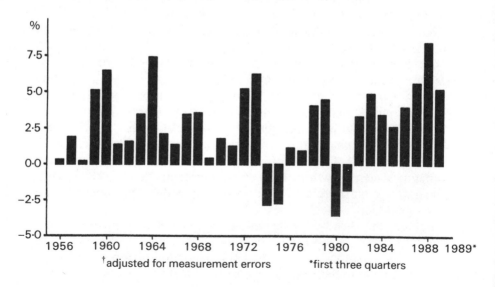

†adjusted for measurement errors   *first three quarters

Chart 3: UK and OECD Demand Growth

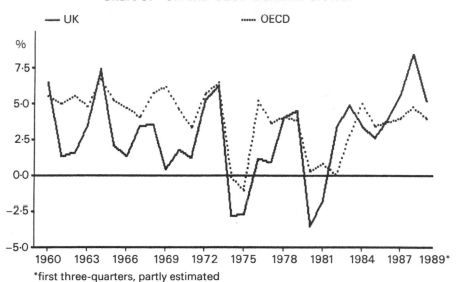

— UK   ····· OECD

*first three-quarters, partly estimated

years (Chart 2). Sheer momentum left demand up by 5 per cent on the year in the first three-quarters of 1989.

Not only was this rate of demand expansion unprecedented in over 30 years of Britain's economic history. It was also wayward judged by international standards. Chart 3 shows the high degree of synchronisation which has existed between the cycle of UK demand and the international demand cycle—where growth on average has been rather stronger. But in 1987-88, this pattern was broken. While the UK enjoyed a cumulative 14-15 per cent demand expansion, the rest of the industrial world achieved 8-9 per cent. So UK demand grew by around 1⅔ times as fast as world demand. And despite the slowdown, UK demand probably outpaced world demand last year as well. Hardly surprisingly, the UK has run up a massive external deficit on current account of the balance of payments. At over 4 per cent of national income, it is a post-war record for the UK and one of the largest in the industrialised world.

In short, the economy has had a major growth accident. It has also had an inflation accident—though not on such a grand scale. The headline retail price inflation number is still uncomfortably close to 8 per cent—double the level of early 1987. But strip out the distorting effect of higher mortgage rates and the jump is more modest—a rise of

TABLE 1

CURRENT ACCOUNT DETERIORATES RAPIDLY

£ billion	1986	1987	1988	1989^e	Change 1986-89
Current account of which	0	−3·8	−14·7	−20·3	−20·3
Visible balance of which	−9·4	−10·9	−20·8	−23·0	−13·6
Food and basics	−6·4	−6·9	−7·8	−7·8	−1·4
Fuel	2·7	2·9	1·6	0·2	−2·5
Semi manufactures	−0·9	−1·9	−3·8	−4·2	−3·3
Finished manufactures	−5·1	−6·0	−11·1	−11·9	−6·7
Total manufactures	−6·1	−7·8	−14·9	−16·0	−10·0
Invisible balance of which	9·3	7·1	6·2	2·7†	−6·6†
Services	6·3	5·7	4·2	4·2†	−2·1†
IPD*	5·2	4·8	5·5	2·4†	−2·8
Transfers	−2·1	−3·4	−3·5	−3·9†	−1·8

Totals subject to rounding error. †Very tentative estimates based on first three-quarters. *Interest, profits and dividends net. ^{e}Inferred from Treasury Autumn Statement forecast.

just 2 per cent, from 4 to 6 per cent. This is a seemingly mild inflation penalty for so wild a boom.

It is an illusion, of course. Thanks to the appreciation of sterling in 1988, the greater part of Britain's excess demand was shipped overseas through the current account. The deterioration here has been suitably widespread—affecting invisible as well as visible trade (Table 1). The invisible surplus fell because of a worse balance on services, especially on tourism, and because of the high interest cost of financing the deficit. On visible trade, the bulk of the deterioration occurred in finished manufactures, especially consumer goods. Had Mr Lawson followed Mr Barber's bad example and forced sterling down to close the trade gap, there is no doubt whatsoever that today's inflation rate would be well into double-digits.

In effect, the current account deficit stands as a hideous symbol of suppressed inflation which could now be rapidly re-imported as sterling crumbles. For this reason, and this reason alone, the deficit remains the single most important barometer of the economy's state of health.

Two Arguments

The previous Chancellor and his now-embattled apologists were prone to two flights of fancy. The first was to argue that the deficit was self-financing. It was, they said, the benign consequence of a private-sector investment boom which could be easily financed on fine terms in the world's long-term capital markets. The evidence wholly discredits this cosy notion. In the course of last year, sterling fell by over 10 per cent despite a further rise in UK interest rates relative to the average of those overseas and an $8-9 billion drain on the reserves.

A key problem is that the capital inflows which have financed the deficit have probably been predominantly short-term, responding, that is, to short-term yield considerations rather than to long-term factors. Although a clear statistical distinction between short- and long-term money is difficult to draw, it is disturbing that those categories of capital flow—direct and portfolio investments—which may be presumed to be of a longer-term nature have registered a net outflow amounting to over £30 billion at an annual rate in the first three-quarters of 1989. As a result, Britain's basic balance-of-payments deficit—the sum of current account and direct plus portfolio capital accounts—probably ran at around 10 per cent of national income last year, the largest hole in recorded history (Chart 4).

Admittedly, there are weaknesses in this measure of the balance of payments. Some portfolio investments, like foreigners' holdings of gilt-edged securities, may be speculative. And the huge balancing item in Britain's balance-of-payments statistics—running at an annualised £15 billion in the first three-quarters of 1989—could conceal some unrecorded long-term capital inflows. But such is the magnitude of the swings recorded that there can be little doubt about the true nature of the capital flows financing the current account. By and large it is 'hot money'.

The problems besetting sterling last year were, then, wholly predictable. We know speculators demand an ever-rising yield inducement for providing a steady inflow of cash to finance a continuing outflow on current account. A one-off rate rise brings largely a once-and-for-all shift in speculative portfolios. For a continuing flow, the interest-rate weapon must be used repeatedly. Speculators demand an even larger yield inducement when prospects

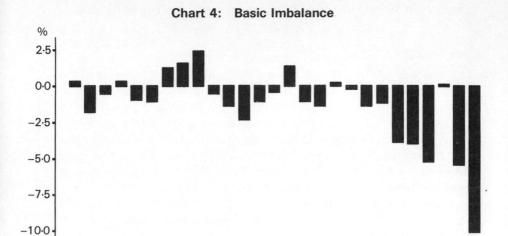

Chart 4:   Basic Imbalance

Current account + direct and portfolio capital accounts as % of GDP.

of growth weaken and attendant political risks rise. And, of course, they want more if they believe German interest rates are about to rise because of the Bundesbank's concern about immigration-induced overheating. When the inducement is not forthcoming, the pound is pummelled.

To this unhappy litany can now be added a further danger. The sharp drop in sterling threatens to inflate Britain's import bill by pushing up import prices. A worse terms of trade might check or even reverse an incipient fall in the deficit, courtesy of improved trade volumes. If so, there could develop a vicious spiral of sterling collapse and inflated deficit.

The other flight of fancy concerned the deficit's self-correcting nature. UK industry, it was suggested, would respond to the challenge of a weaker home market by redoubling exporting effort and competing more effectively with imports. Domestic demand would fall but—hey presto!—net exports would rise—so the onshore economy would continue to grow at its trend 3 per cent rate while the deficit came down. *Self-correction meant painless correction.*

There is one snag with this seductive idea. It has never happened that way before. Even in principle, the argument could not apply to that large, mainly non-manufacturing, sector of the economy which

TABLE 2

EXPORT VOLUME TRENDS, EXCLUDING OIL

Per cent growth (year on year)		1970-87 p.a.	1988	1989 Q1	1989 Q2	1989 Q3	1989 Year[e]
Goods and services of which:		3·5	2·0	10·1	6·0	8·0	9¼
services	(0·27)	3·1	−1·3	2·6	1·4	3·2	3¼
goods	(0·73)	3·7	3·3	13·2	7·8	9·7	11½
of which:							
manufactures	(0·63)	3·5	6·5	14·6	7·8	9·2	n.a.
of which:							
semis§	(0·23)	3·9	5·9	6·3	2·6	0·0	n.a.
finished§	(0·40)	3·3	6·1	17·4	12·2	14·0	n.a.
of which:							
consumer§		3·4	−0·6	20·8	18·5	16·4	n.a.
capital§		2·5	18·1	24·6	14·0	11.2	n.a.
other finished§		3·8	0·7	11·0	7·7	14·2	n.a.

§Ex-erratics.   [e]Treasury Autumn Statement estimate, services inferred.
Figures in brackets show 1988 share in ex-oil exports (incl. erratics).

Chart 5: Capital Utilisation Falling But Still High

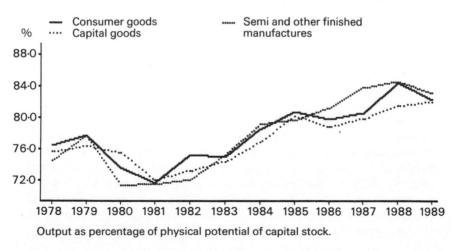

Output as percentage of physical potential of capital stock.

TABLE 3

TABLE 3

IMPORT PENETRATION STILL RISING[†]

1956-70	1971-79	1980-88	1987	1988	1989	
					Q1-Q3	Year[e]
1·8	3·6	2·2	1·6	1·6	2·0	2·4

[†]Growth in volume of imports of goods and services divided by growth in domestic demand, net of indirect taxes and adjusted for measurement errors. Ex-oil imports post-1970.   [e]Inferred from Autumn Statement forecast.

does not engage extensively in international trade. And unpalatable reality shows that it does not really work for manufacturing industry either. The various industrial surveys reveal a fall in confidence and a slump in output expectations.

It is interesting to note that this overall slowdown in activity has occurred despite a surprising and welcome jump in export volumes. Britain's share of its export markets apparently increased in 1989. Some commentators have suggested that gains in competitiveness consequent on sterling's fall are responsible. But this is unlikely. On average, competitiveness merely stabilised last year. And the claimed response is implausibly fast.

The Treasury has no doubt that this export bonus is explained by the release of capacity pressures which, in 1988, caused a diversion of potential exports to the home market. Table 2 and Chart 5 provide some support for this view. The dramatic recovery in export volumes occurs in consumer goods and intermediate manufactures whose capacity utilisation rates have fallen most from particularly high levels.

But matters are not so clear-cut. Import volumes have also been surprisingly strong. Import penetration—imports relative to domestic demand—has surged, despite the easing of capacity pressure. In 1989, import volumes, excluding oil, may have increased at nearly 2½ times the growth in domestic demand—rather above the average relationship over the 1980s (Table 3).

Even more puzzling, the unexpected buoyancy of import growth is most marked in precisely the same areas (consumer goods, finished intermediates) where export performance has been unusually good (Table 4). Why should the volume of imports of consumer goods, ex-cars, be rising by over 13 per cent year on year when consumers' expenditure is up by only 4 per cent? It is almost as if UK producers have deserted the UK to seek more succulent pastures overseas,

TABLE 4

IMPORT VOLUME TRENDS, EXCLUDING OIL

Per cent growth (year on year)		1970-87 p.a.	1988	Q1	1989 Q2	Q3	Year[e]
Goods and services of which:		5·3	13·3	15·6	8·1	8·1	9
services	(0·2)	3·5	9·4	11·0	3·1	6·5	3¾
goods	(0·8)	5·9	14·2	16·8	9·3	8·4	10¼
of which:							
manufactures	(0·65)	8·1	18·0	19·8	10·3	12·0	n.a.
of which:							
semis[§]	(0·23)	6·4	12·8	12·7	6·1	5·9	n.a.
finished	(0·42)	10·5	19·1	25·3	15·3	15·0	n.a.
of which:							
consumer[§]		11·4	15·9	22·8	12·0	15·9	n.a.
capital[§]		10·4	23·8	26·8	21.9	15.8	n.a.
other finished[§]		10·3	18·7	24·6	14·2	13·7	n.a.

[§]Ex-erratics.   [e]Treasury Autumn Statement estimate, services inferred.
Figures in brackets show 1988 share in ex-oil imports (incl. erratics).

leaving the home market wide open to the foreign competition. But this is hardly a compelling explanation.

The precise role played by capacity pressures remains unresolved. The big picture remains perfectly clear. The performance of net exports is dominated by the movement in UK demand relative to overseas demand—with competitiveness factors also playing a role from time to time. As Chart 6 shows, the ratio of import to export volume has moved up consistently with the rise in the UK's relative level of demand. The relationship apparently broke down in 1979-81— when net imports did not fall sharply despite a large fall in UK demand. But this is easily explained by the severe loss of competitiveness which then occurred. On this logic, the trade deficit will stay high even if UK demand moderates and grows at the industrial world rate. Indeed, in such circumstances, the deficit could deteriorate further for two reasons.

First, even if exports and imports grow at the same rate, there will be a tendency for the absolute gap to increase, simply because imports are

Chart 6: Trade Dominated by Relative Demand

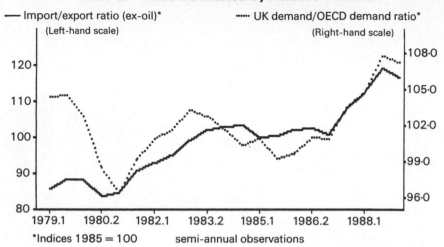

— Import/export ratio (ex-oil)*
(Left-hand scale)

······ UK demand/OECD demand ratio*
(Right-hand scale)

*Indices 1985 = 100   semi-annual observations

well in excess of exports. Imports of goods and services are nearly 20 per cent larger than exports. Therefore, if imports grow by 10 per cent, exports must grow by around 12 per cent just to stabilise the deficit.

Second, more pessimistic observers contend that the UK has a structural trade deficit, courtesy of an unfavourable set of trade elasticities. The response of imports to increases in UK domestic demand appears to exceed the corresponding response of UK exports to increases in overseas domestic demand. But according to an OECD study, although the gap is particularly unfavourable for UK manufactures, it is small for all goods and services (Table 5).

These ideas can be broadly captured by a relationship which links the net non-oil trade balance to levels of relative demand and a measure of competitiveness. Although over-simplified, it produces an

TABLE 5

IMPORT ELASTICITY LESS EXPORT ELASTICITY[†]

	USA	Japan	WG	France	UK	Italy	Canada
Goods and services	0·11	−0·29	−0·25	−0·11	0·10	0·36	0·19
Manufactures	0·18	−0·32	−0·24	−0·01	0·25	0·81	0·15

[†]Import elasticity with respect to domestic demand minus export elasticity with respect to world domestic demand.

Source: Economies in Transition, Paris: OECD, 1989.

Chart 7: The Imperative of Slower UK Demand Growth

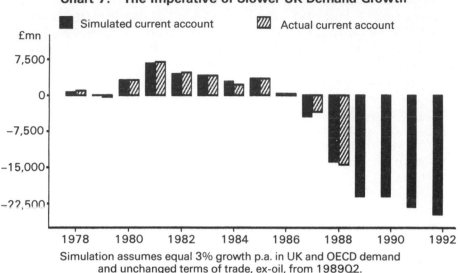

■ Simulated current account   ▨ Actual current account

Simulation assumes equal 3% growth p.a. in UK and OECD demand
and unchanged terms of trade, ex-oil, from 1989Q2.

impressive track of Britain's deficit over the last decade. And, as Chart 7 shows, the UK's projected deficit gets larger if UK demand and world demand grow in line. Clearly, this is not a sustainable position.

Against this background, consider the magnitude of the UK's problem. What would have to happen to demand this year to eradicate a £20 billion current account deficit at a stroke? The answer is that domestic demand might have to fall by 8 per cent—sufficient to produce the requisite fall in imports. GDP might fall by around 4 per cent.

In practice, adjustment would be less abrupt and less brutal. It is only necessary for UK demand to fall relative to world demand over a period of time. So to an extent, the world can take the weight off the UK's shoulders by boosting British exports. It is, therefore, indeed fortunate that world activity appears so well supported. The decoupling of the US and European growth cycles is a blessing which holds the promise of a reasonable 2½-3 per cent rate of industrial world expansion. *The prospect of good world growth is one of the major safeguards against outright recession in the UK and greatly distinguishes this episode from the dark days of 1980-81.* Even so, the UK may still have to endure absolute falls in domestic demand with very little expansion of GDP for several years.

11

Sterling and Inflation

In principle, it seems that the fall in sterling offers a more palatable way out. The exchange rate decline, artfully engineered by chancellors past and present, provides a classic correction mechanism. High interest rates have achieved domestic expenditure reduction; a competitiveness boost should help switch production into net exports. My short answer to this line of thought is 'yes, but'. Yes, it was wholly appropriate that the exchange rate should fall. But it is also essential to ensure that the economy has the capacity to absorb the boost to competitiveness. Otherwise, inflation will stick or even rise.

And here we come to the other legacy of the Lawson boom. In all likelihood, the UK is still suffering from capacity deficiency and, regrettably, a too-low level of unemployment. The clearest sign of this difficulty is the continued escalation of pay. Private sector settlements have risen from 5-6 per cent at the beginning of the boom to over 8 per cent in the third quarter of 1989. Total earnings, which comprise settlements plus overtime and bonuses, have run from 7½ per cent to over 9 per cent.

The Government hopes there will be a spontaneous moderation of pay settlements. But this is wholly improbable. More likely, private sector settlements will rise towards 10 per cent in the months ahead—for several reasons. *First*, many workers feel 'short-changed' by the jump in inflation during 1989. They will seek compensation for this unexpected cut in their real wages. *Second*, there is a great deal of pay emulation in today's labour market. The 9-9½ per cent settlements reached last summer and the current disputed claims in the motor and engineering industries are acting as a beacon for others. *Finally*, and most importantly, unemployment continues to fall. The labour market is tightening. Employers are in the unenviable position of facing labour shortages at precisely the moment when they need staff to man their newly installed machines. Who, in this environment, would want to be the first Gradgrind employer to press down on pay and engage in a strike?

The impact of the upward pressure on pay is made considerably more potent by the downward pressure on *productivity*. Unit labour costs are therefore escalating in just the manner textbooks say they should in the first part of the cycle downphase. In the onshore economy, unit labour costs have jumped from 2 per cent growth in early 1987 to around 8 per cent in the late summer of 1989. In the first quarter of this year, they could be up by 9 per cent. To curb unit labour

Chart 8: Output Gap

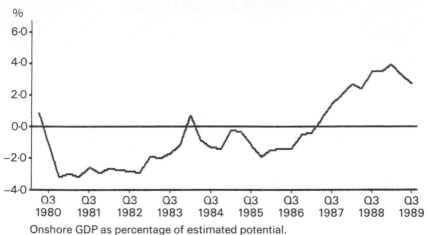

Onshore GDP as percentage of estimated potential.

cost inflation seriously, unemployment, I suggest, must rise. But that cannot be engineered without a great deal of output pain. The labour supply is growing very slowly—perhaps at ¼ per cent a year. The growth in jobs must therefore fall to a ¼ per cent merely to stabilise unemployment. To get unemployment up, employment will have to fall. This dramatic change in labour market conditions implies a period of at best very weak output growth and depressed profits.

Chart 8 shows another way of making the same point. The IMF, which has an unenviable facility for jargon, calls this chart an output gap. It relates the level of onshore GDP to an estimate of the economy's potential level of output. Potential output is a slippery concept. But, for simplicity's sake, it can be thought of as the level of output which could be sustained for a significant period with the men and machines at industry's disposal and given its general level of efficiency.

Inevitably, the estimates are a little soft. They tell, nevertheless, a very interesting tale about the whole of the 1980s. This is that the 1980-81 recession, the deepest since the 1930s, dug a deep hole—the economy plunged well below potential. Subsequently that hole, coupled with improving rates of productivity, allowed the economy to enjoy a steady rate of advance to the end of 1986 without experiencing any marked inflation or balance-of-payments difficulty. For practically the whole of this period, the economy operated below potential. North Sea oil also helped, of course. However, Britain's big boom

13

TABLE 6
TABLE 6
MONEY MODEL SIMULATIONS

	1990	1991	1992
A) *10% money growth, fixed competitiveness*			
Inflation	6	4½	3½
GDP growth, ex-oil	¾	2½	3½
Domestic demand growth	1	3¼	5
Current account (% GDP)	-3¾	-4¾	-6½
B) *10% money growth, 5% competitiveness gain*			
Inflation	6¾	7	7
GDP growth, ex-oil	1	2¾	3¼
Domestic demand growth	¾	1¾	2½
Current account (% GDP)	-3¾	-2¾	-2
C) *Falling money growth, 5% competitiveness gain*			
Inflation	6½	5	3¼
GDP growth, ex-oil	½	1¾	2¾
Domestic demand growth	-1	-¼	1½
Current account (% GDP)	-2¾	-1½	-½

Notes: Inflation measured by domestic demand deflator. Simulations assume around 3% p.a. growth in world demand and in UK productive potential, ex-oil. Cases A and B assume 10% M2 growth, Case C assumes a declining money growth path: 7%, 6%, 5% in 1990, 1991, 1992 respectively. A measure of trade competitiveness is assumed to remain unchanged from its end-1989 level in Case A but to improve by 5% p.a. from 1990 in Cases B and C. The current account figures assume a recovery in oil output in 1990 and a generally small positive surplus on the balance of interest, profit and dividends less transfers. Cases B and C incorporate modest terms of trade losses.

subsequently pushed activity well above the level—around 3 per cent on our 'guesstimate'—warranted by its underlying efficiency.

It is a reasonable conjecture that all this excess will have to be taken out before inflationary pressures truly subside. That, in turn, implies a growth rate which is well below Britain's long-term potential—which could also be 3 per cent or so—over the next couple of years.

Table 6 attempts to add some figures to this analysis using the results of simulations on a very simple monetarist model. It is monetarist in the sense that the growth in real money supply is the main motor of domestic demand. Otherwise it has very conventional properties. For example, the model shows that a rise in demand boosts output and spills over into extra imports. If output increases in relation to the economy's potential then inflation tends to accelerate, in turn, influencing the growth of real money supply. I have found this simple structure helpful in understanding the growth and inflation performance of the economy through the 1980s.

The simulations assume as background that world growth and UK potential run at around 3 per cent a year. The model produces forecasts for onshore growth and inflation—measured by an index akin to retail prices excluding mortgage interest. Regrettably, the model does not fully articulate the current account so the figures shown in Table 6 have been produced as much by hand as by computer. Nevertheless, they give a feel for orders of magnitude. The simulations make varying assumptions about exchange rate policy—which helps determine Britain's international competitiveness—and monetary growth. Money is measured by the M2 aggregate comprising cash and retail bank and building society deposits.

o **Case A** examines the implications of monetary growth continuing at today's rate (around 10 per cent for M2) and a fixed level of competitiveness. Although superficially attractive in terms of output growth and inflation, the results are built on sand. The external deficit gets progressively larger as demand growth persists at too high a rate.

o **Case B** responds to Case A's difficulty by assuming a boost to competitiveness—5 per cent a year between 1990 and 1992. This produces a better but hardly spectacular trade performance. Just as damning, it leaves inflation stuck at 7 per cent.

o **Case C** accordingly assumes an extra degree of credit restraint, producing a more marked fall in demand and output. The package works, eventually. By 1992, the economy has atoned for its previous excesses. The current account is tolerably low and growth and inflation are within a margin of error of 3 per cent apiece. But the road to redemption is decidedly rocky. This year (1990), the underlying rate of inflation rises to 6½ per cent despite a mere ½ per cent growth in GDP and a 1 per cent fall in domestic demand.

On this analysis, the long-term goal of steady growth with low inflation is attainable. But to succeed, three types of adjustment are required. The economy must secure:

o *A fall in GDP growth relative to the economy's potential*, probably implying no more than 1-1½ per cent onshore growth on average in 1990-91.

o *A fall in domestic demand growth in the UK relative to demand growth overseas.* Over the next two years, UK demand may well have to fall *absolutely* on a scale only exceeded in the great recessions of the mid-1970s and early 1980s.

o *An improvement in competitiveness to help switch production into net exporting activity.* A 5 per cent per annum gain in competitiveness may be the maximum absorbable by the economy without intolerable inflationary difficulty.

Will the Economy Adjust?

The next question is whether the economy will so adjust of its own volition. If not, policy will have to change to prod the economy back on track. Of the three conditions, the suggested improvement in competitiveness is the least of the Chancellor's headaches. *Without any further fall from the current level (index:87), sterling would register a decline of around 6 per cent this year—delivering the best part of a 5 per cent competitiveness gain even allowing for the UK's differentially high rate of unit labour cost inflation.*

The biggest question-mark hangs over the evolution of domestic demand. In recent years, the common error among economic forecasters has been to under-estimate the strength of demand. But after more than 12 months of high interest rates it may now be right to project a marked curtailment of spending. To me, the forces of deflation appear pretty intense.

An indication of this is the tightness of domestic monetary policy. There are, of course, no perfect measures. But one upon which some weight can be placed is the level of real interest rates. On a prospective 12-month inflation rate of 5 per cent, today's base rates are close to double digits in real, pre-tax terms—possibly the highest since the early 1930s (Chart 9). *I suggest that, for this and other reasons, it would be bizarre to conclude that monetary policy was anything but extremely tight. This squeeze should now impinge increasingly on expenditure decisions both by households and by companies.*

Consumer spending, though slowing down, surprised many respectable forecasters by its strength last year. In 1989, consumption grew by over 4 per cent. The main reason for this buoyancy, which really

Chart 9: Real Prospective Base Rates

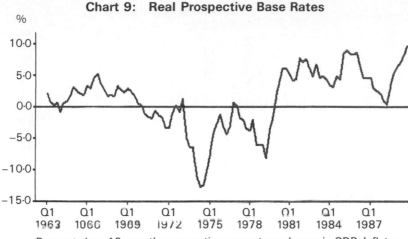

Base rate less 12-month prospective percentage change in GDP deflator.

should not have come as a surprise, is time lags. It takes a long time for a monetary squeeze to feed through to the consumer.

One of the main linkages is likely to come through the housing market. Although the relationship is coarse, there has been an association between rising housing wealth and the fall in household saving. Rising wealth meant people were more willing to take on debt to finance extra spending. In 1989, the lagged effects of the housing boom were still depressing saving. But, thanks to the fall in house prices, we now have the prospect of some rise in saving. Consumer spending may therefore grow by a mere 1 per cent this year.

Company expenditure may fare even worse—and actually fall. One aspect of the monetary squeeze is the development of a huge company sector deficit. The deficit measures the difference between retained profits and expenditure on stocks and investments. On official figures, it could run out at around £18 billion or so in 1989. Expressed as a percentage of profits, the deficit is in excess of the level seen in 1974 when most observers agree British industry went belly up (Chart 10). It is unlikely, however, to be as bad as in 1974. Unlike then, a significant proportion of this deficit was probably *planned* by companies. The boom of 1987-88 exposed the deficiency of the capital stock. Meanwhile, structural improvements in balance sheets—lower gearing in particular—and the 1987 crash encouraged more recourse to bank finance. Such considerations help explain the unusually prolonged nature of the company sector deficit.

17

Chart 10: Companies in Deficit

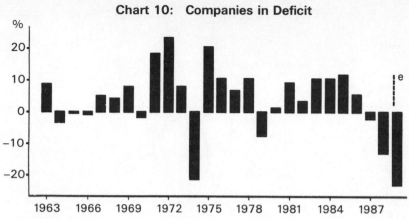

Company saving less investment as percentage of profits (ex-oil after 1969).
e1989 estimate.

The scale of the deficit, however, is probably an accident. The unprecedented boom of 1987-88 appears to have encouraged companies to entertain unrealistic hopes for market expansion upon which investment plans were based. The loss of credibility of the Government's counter-inflation programme has probably had a similar insidious effect. Companies delayed adjustment in the expectation that political pressures would prompt a timely relaxation of policy. Although a reasonable interpretation of the political process, this happy belief discouraged companies from taking an appropriately tough line in pay negotiations. As a result, inflation has become embedded, forcing the Government to tighten economic policy. Companies, in turn, have found themselves marooned with rising stock levels and with extravagant investment commitments predicated on assumptions of market growth which are no longer plausible. In the post-war era, companies generally ran financial surpluses and turned around such deficits as occurred very quickly by cutting stocks. The same will surely happen this time.

Although the official figures are of doubtful quality, survey evidence supports the view that companies have experienced an involuntary build-up of stocks as demand has fallen. The stock-output ratio in the whole economy appears to have run well above its previous downtrend (Chart 11). If industry were to attempt to return to the old trend, a £5 billion or more shake-out of stocks this year could be implied. The implied swing in stocks between 1989 and 1990 would be over £10 billion—in excess of the swing seen in the 1980 recession.

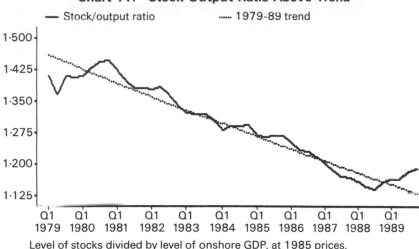

Chart 11: Stock Output Ratio Above Trend

—— Stock/output ratio ⋯⋯ 1979-89 trend

Level of stocks divided by level of onshore GDP, at 1985 prices.

The collective attempt to push the stock-output ratio down would fail, however, as inventory cuts cascaded through the economy. One purchaser's cut in stocks is another supplier's involuntary stock build-up. The impact would be a depression of output and a rise in the stock-output ratio. This in turn would prompt a further round of stock-shedding. In this way, a large stock shake-out could precipitate absolute falls in GDP. *Although its scale is difficult to gauge, the stock cycle has the potential to be a major deflationary force.*

Industry is also likely to react to the monetary squeeze by cutting *investment.* The evidence for this comes directly from industrial surveys in which recorded investment intentions have fallen dramatically (Chart 12). Business investment might decline by 4-5 per cent this year.

Implications for Policy

In short, I conclude that economic policy may now be tight enough to deliver the fall in domestic demand required to cut the trade deficit and curtail inflation, but that we cannot be sure; that the pressures may be more keenly felt by the company sector than by the personal sector; that this implies the possibility of cutbacks in investment with undesirable implications for the industrial base; that sterling's fall is now bordering on the excessive; that the government's loss of counter-inflation credibility

19

Chart 12: Investment Intentions and Outturn

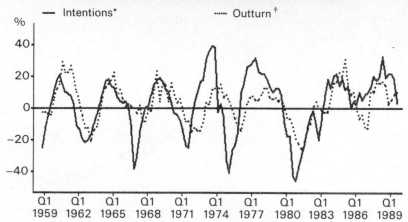

— Intentions*   ⋯⋯ Outturn†

*Balance of CBI respondents indicating more investment.
†Percentage growth in manufacturing investment (recent data are tentative).

may have discouraged companies from taking a tougher line in pay bargaining and that this has probably increased the output and unemployment cost of getting inflation down. If these views are accepted, several policy implications follow.

There is, first, the question of the appropriate *mix of fiscal and monetary policy*. Recent public debate has focussed on whether the Government will or should tighten fiscal policy. In principle, more active use of the tax weapon would afford Mr Major that extra policy instrument required to hit simultaneously two policy objectives. Higher taxation would enable him to reduce domestic spending; lower interest rates meanwhile could be used to engineer a fall in sterling, boosting competitiveness and net exports. This prescription provides for a classic expenditure-reducing, output-switching mix appropriate for an economy suffering from deficient capacity and an unsupportable external deficit.

Despite the theoretical attractions, the case for a major tightening of fiscal policy—implying a higher budget surplus—appears weak. The immediate priority is to stabilise sterling, not to encourage a further fall. Higher base rates required for purposes of exchange rate management would also reinforce the squeeze on domestic demand. In circumstances of sterling flight, the same instrument—interest rates—serves all policy purposes. *Major fiscal deflation would smack of overkill for no good reason.*

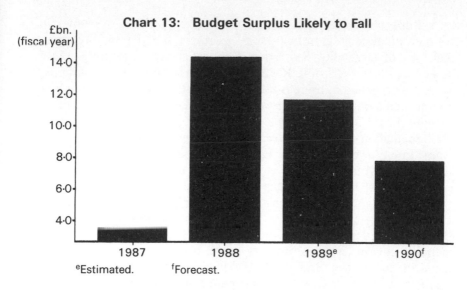

Chart 13: Budget Surplus Likely to Fall

£bn. (fiscal year)

eEstimated.   fForecast.

In practice, the greater likelihood is that fiscal policy will ease this year, largely the result of normal cyclical stabilisers. The budget surplus is planned to fall and probably will, caught between the updraft of higher public spending (boosted, in part, by rising unemployment) and the downdraft of lower growth and tax take (Chart 13). Native caution laced with residual concern that demand will yet again outpace Treasury forecasts may prompt the Chancellor, rightly in my view, to limit but not prevent such a decline in the budget surplus. In practical terms, it might mean not indexing income tax allowances—an implicit boost to the exchequer of £1·5 billion. A more generous stance could be recommended only if there emerged in the Budget run-up overwhelming evidence of a monstrous collapse of domestic demand.

A second policy issue concerns the likely *composition of demand*. It is not within the Government's power to pre-determine the split of demand in the economy between consumption and investment. These expenditure components are interdependent and the policy instruments available to prise them apart are not particularly powerful. Within the limitations, a case can be made on grounds of preserving industrial capacity for a twist in policy, attempting to favour industry over households, investment over consumption. The obvious option would be a staged reduction in the corporation tax rate towards the income tax rate, a measure which would support investment and promote greater neutrality of the tax system.

21

A third policy concern is the *credibility* of the Government's counter-inflation programme. Most observers would probably agree that loss of credibility has reduced the chances of securing lower inflation without recession. Regrettably, there are no instant solutions. To restore reputation, there is frankly no substitute for the long slog of establishing a track record of low inflation. Many European Monetary System (EMS) advocates hope that Britain could painlessly import such reputation from the Germans, a proposition of questionable merit. In any event, early full EMS membership appears unlikely. In current circumstances, a more fruitful line of inquiry concerns the presentation of monetary policy.

It has long been a nonsense that the only targeted measure of money supply is narrow money, M0. On the admission of the previous Chancellor, M0 amounts to little more than a coincident indicator of spending in cash terms—a property which hardly warrants its elevated status in the Budget Red Book. If M0 is to continue as a targeted measure, it should at least keep company with a new target for broad money. This would be all the more appropriate since it was Mr Lawson's indifference to the broader aggregates which contributed so much to the policy accident of 1987-88.

The choice of measure would be important. M4 should probably be ruled out on the grounds that it is too severely distorted by shifts in wholesale money deposits. The main candidates are a money services index which gives weight to components of money according to their potential 'spendability'—the idealist's choice—or M2, which would find favour amongst simpler practitioners like myself.

Whatever Mr Major decides, his overriding priority now should be to stabilise sterling. Sterling's fall is not only a threat to the Government's short-term inflation objectives. There is a distinct risk of the economy becoming locked into a vicious circle of devaluation and rising pay. If so, the economy would be condemned to the worst of hard landings—several years of not-so-mild stagflation. Despite encouraging signs of adjustment in the economy, the case for shock therapy remains compelling. If sterling were to suffer imminently another sharp slide, the Chancellor should raise base rates again.

Subject to the proviso that Mr Major keeps up the pressure, I expect to see a growth recession in 1990, with the possibility of one or two quarters of falling activity (Chart 14). Ex-oil growth falls from 3-3½ per cent in 1989 to just a fraction in 1990. Subsequently, I offer redemption. In 1991 onshore growth recovers to 2 per cent—thanks to

Chart 14: Growth and Inflation Prospects

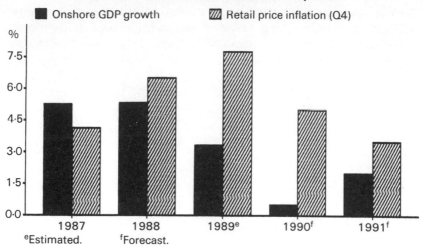

■ Onshore GDP growth   ▨ Retail price inflation (Q4)

Chart 15: Current Account Deficit Set to Fall

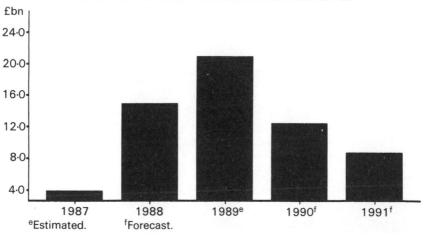

the easing of current account and inflation constraints. The current account deficit could fall to £12-13 billion in 1990 (Chart 15). And inflation, after a short-run upward blip, should fall to 5 per cent by the end of 1990—with the prospect of a still lower rate thereafter (Chart 14). Although just a glimmer in the forecaster's eye, 1991 inflation might benefit from the flattering effect of low mortgage rates as interest rates fall.

Thanks then to the cracking of company and consumer confidence, there is the possibility of an almost surgical solution to the economy's difficulties: not the living death of not-so-mild stagflation—more a restorative jolt to the system which might just re-synchronise the election and business cycles.

2

WHAT WENT WRONG WITH UK DEMAND AND TRADE PERFORMANCE? HOW TO PUT IT RIGHT?
Giles Keating
Credit Suisse First Boston Ltd.

Introduction

MONETARY POLICY is 'what went wrong' with demand and trade performance in the UK. Monetary policy was far too expansionary from around early 1987, and as a direct consequence the exchange rate was too low and asset prices rose too fast. I will make three key points on this:

1. The problem was not exchange rate targeting as such, but the choice of too low a rate;

2. The erroneous choice of this low rate stemmed right back to early 1987 and the excess monetary expansion began then;

3. The housing market was the key transmission mechanism from monetary policy on to consumer spending.

Recent History of Demand and Trade Performance

I will begin by reminding you of the recent history of UK demand and trade performance. Back in 1986, demand and output were approximately in line. The current account started that year with a good surplus which had disappeared by the end of the year, the decline essentially reflecting the collapse of oil prices. The non-oil account showed a small deficit (Chart 1).

Chart 1: UK Current Account Balance
As a Percentage of GDP

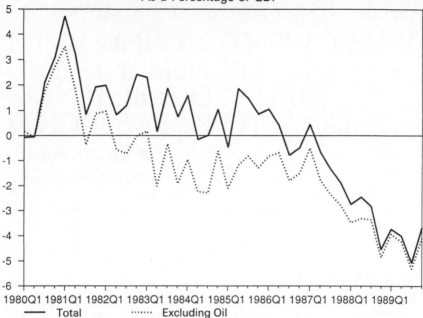

——— Total   ⋯⋯⋯ Excluding Oil

Demand and output began to move out of line during 1987, and the gap between the two grew at an accelerating rate in 1988 (Chart 2). Real domestic demand grew by 17·5 per cent in total over the two years to the end of 1988; GDP was up by just 8·3 per cent.

Arithmetically, this growing excess of demand over output had to be reflected in a worsening external position. The current account registered a growing deficit during 1987 and then widened rapidly throughout 1988.

During 1989, growth of demand gradually slowed to a virtual standstill, but growth of output also declined, so the current account has broadly stabilised.

Excess Demand was the Problem

The fact that the trade problem really emerged in 1988, when output was still growing strongly, suggests that the UK's economic problem stems from excessive growth in demand, rather than poor production performance or poor trade performance.

26

Chart 2: GDP and Domestic Demand
Index 1986Q1 = 100

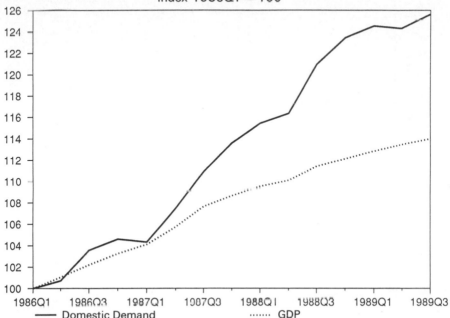

— Domestic Demand ······· GDP

Consistent with this view, export market shares have held up well (Chart 3). However, import market shares have risen sharply (Chart 4). But this rise in import shares has occurred despite sterling's tendency to be correctly valued or undervalued relative to its purchasing power parity (PPP) level (Chart 5). So unless there has been a sudden worsening in non-price factors—and I am not aware of evidence for this—the higher import shares are simply the result of excessive domestic demand. They reflect demand rising far faster than output, with capacity constraints and the price mechanism pushing that excess demand into imports.

Causes of Excess Demand: Monetary Policy

Once we accept that excess demand was the problem, the task is to look for causes. I am going to do this from the angle of exchange rate policy, which was of great importance at the time.

It will be recalled that sterling moved largely in the DM3·60-3·90 range from mid-1982 through to late 1985. Then came the oil price shock, with prices initially halving from around $30 per barrel to around $15, and then by mid-1986 falling to a low below $10. Sterling

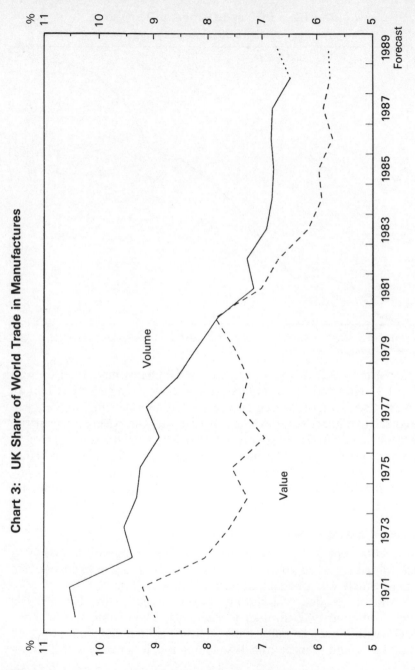

Chart 3: UK Share of World Trade in Manufactures

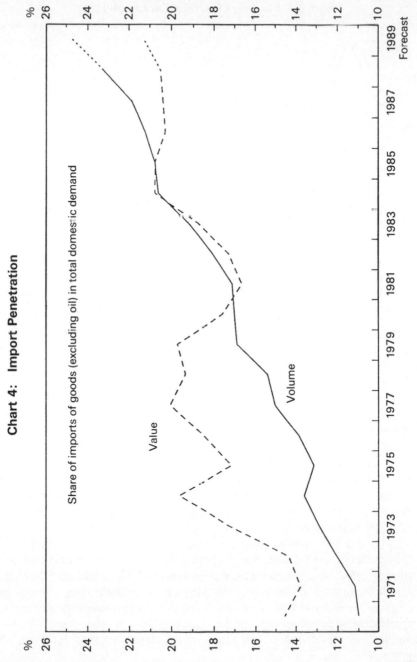

Chart 4: Import Penetration

Share of imports of goods (excluding oil) in total domestic demand

Chart 5: Sterling Effective Exchange Rate

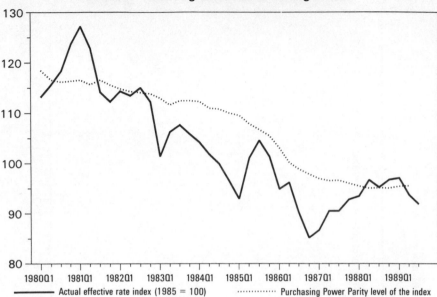

Actual effective rate index (1985 = 100) .... Purchasing Power Parity level of the index

went with them. The currency plunged precipitously, particularly against the deutschemark and the yen, in late 1985 and throughout much of 1986. The DM rate reached a low in the 2·70s in early 1987 (Chart 6).

Then the foreign exchange markets began to have second thoughts, and started to push the pound up. One reason was that oil prices had rebounded from their lows. Another reason was, perhaps, that market participants started to feel that the gloom surrounding sterling had been overdone; the economy was not that dependent on oil.

However, the UK Government had other ideas. The authorities began to intervene heavily to hold the currency down. Chart 7 shows the scale of this intervention, and reminds us what a change this was from previous policy.

Why did the Government try to cap sterling then, at the start of 1987, when the DM rate was around DM 2·70 to the pound and the sterling effective exchange rate was around 85? They had no particular metric to justify the choice of this rate, except perhaps that it was at or close to an all-time low. The choice of this absurd rate represents the greatest tragedy of policy in the Lawson era. It was crazily below purchasing power parity (PPP) against the deutschemark, far more so

Chart 6: Sterling-Deutschemark: Actual and PPP
DM per £

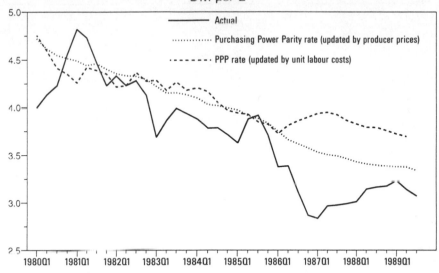

Actual
.... Purchasing Power Parity rate (updated by producer prices)
-------- PPP rate (updated by unit labour costs)

Chart 7: UK Underlying Change in Reserves
US$ Billion

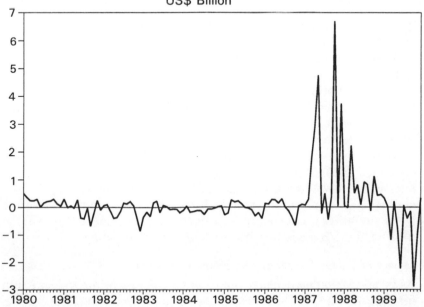

Chart 8: Real Interest Rates

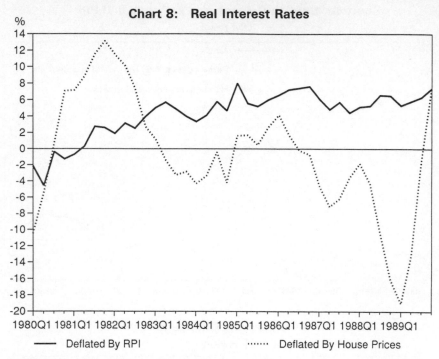

%

Deflated By RPI   ······· Deflated By House Prices

than at any time in the 1980s, and also greatly undervalued against PPP on the effective rate. It was a policy bound to lead ultimately to monetary excess.

Why could the Government not have accepted that the market, having overshot on the downside following the oil price shock, was in process of groping its way to an equilibrium level? Why not allow that process to work itself out before trying to stabilise the currency? Why target a rate so far from measured PPP?

From then on, the road to ruin is well charted. Intervention continued on a massive scale throughout 1987 and much of 1988. Interest rates were cut without domestic justification. The October 1987 stock market crash confused the picture for a while, but cannot excuse the UK's continuing to cut rates in May 1988, when the Federal Reserve (the 'Fed') and the Bundesbank had started to tighten again.

Causes of Excess Demand: The Housing Market

Asset prices, and particularly house prices, were a prime transmission mechanism for this monetary expansion. Even on the crude,

Chart 9: Ratio of House Prices to Underlying Earnings
Index 1985Q1 = 100

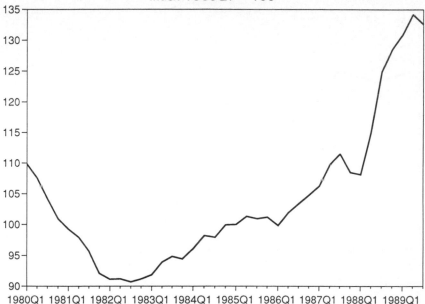

backward-looking basis used in Chart 8, the real interest cost of buying houses was negative throughout 1987 and more so as the housing boom accelerated in early 1988.

The effect on the house price to earnings ratio was disastrous. It accelerated smartly in 1987 to reach a peak level for the 1980s, and then after a pause following the Crash it rose at an incredible rate (Chart 9).

The advance announcement of the ending of multiple mortgage relief also contributed, although the macro-economic effect of the 1988 Budget was deflationary (Chart 10).

The influence of this asset price inflation on consumer behaviour in a deregulated financial system has been well analysed by John Muellbauer and ourselves.[1] Consumers are able to release their increased wealth via a massive increase in borrowing, which does not seem unsustainable to them or to the lenders because of the massive amount of equity in their homes.

---

[1] See M. Franklin, G. Keating, J. Muellbauer and A. Murphy, 'Why Has UK Personal Saving Collapsed?', Credit Suisse First Boston (CSFB), mimeo, July 1989, and references therein.

Chart 10: PSBR Excluding Privatisation Proceeds
Percentage of GDP

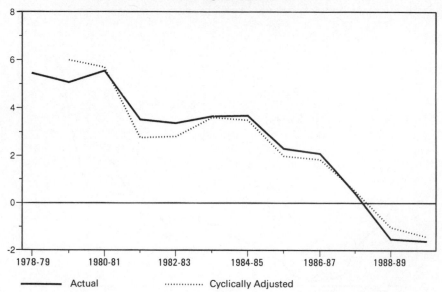

Actual ⸻ Cyclically Adjusted ⋯⋯⋯⋯

In answering the question 'What went wrong with demand and trade performance?', I conclude that excessive monetary expansion due to a misguidedly low exchange rate target led to asset price inflation, particularly in housing. This boosted consumer spending, in a way not previously experienced because house prices had not previously been so high during the period of deregulated consumer lending. Growth of consumption, a long way ahead of growth of productive potential, led to a rapidly deteriorating current account and higher import penetration, despite a good performance by UK producers who broadly maintained export market share.

How To Put It Right?

What can be done to correct this situation? The problem is worsened by two factors:

1. The wealth effect on consumer spending is remarkably long-lasting; even with house prices now edging down, spending is still being buoyed up by all the equity in homes.

2. Any move to correct the problem by bringing house prices down really sharply will meet powerful political resistance from voters

who abhor being left with an asset worth less than the loan they took out to pay for it.

There is no absolute solution; it is a matter of balancing these and related problems. My preferred solution is thus a hybrid: earnings inflation must be allowed to erode the house price to earnings ratio, while nominal house prices are made to fall only very slowly and then stabilise; interest rates must be set at the level which achieves this type of path for nominal house prices, while simultaneously preventing the exchange rate from falling any further, for that would boost earnings growth more. Indeed, ideally, the exchange rate should rise somewhat. This prescription involves using interest rates for two objectives, and should these be incompatible, I propose a second instrument: Exchange Rate Mechanism (ERM) entry, but this time at a sensible, high rate, preferably at or around DM3, to add to credibility and thus reduce the interest-rate level required to defend any particular exchange-rate level.[2]

A fiscal tightening is not appropriate—in contrast to 1981. That is because the exchange rate is currently too low (it was overvalued in 1981), so we do not want the lower interest rates implied by tighter fiscal policy. However, fiscal policy may have a different role. If the pain of falling house prices becomes too large politically, then mortgage relief should be increased. This is not desirable in itself but as an evil it is preferable to having interest rates too low.

---

[2] Entry at this high rate is possible even if sterling's spot rate is lower at the time of joining. Say sterling is trading in the low 2·80s against the DM, then entry to the ERM at a central rate of 3·00, with a 6 per cent band, would be possible. The capital inflows that would follow sterling's entry, due to increased confidence in the UK's policies, would then drive sterling up to around or above its central rate, *instead* of causing an undesirable cut in interest rates.

3

BRITISH INDUSTRIAL POLICY FOR THE 1990s

Walter Eltis
Director General,
The National Economic Development Office

WHAT SHOULD WE SEEK from industrial policy in the 1990s? After a brief summary of the degree of industrial recovery that has been achieved since 1979 and what has not been achieved, this paper will discuss what government can contribute in two principal areas, research and development and training where it is widely agreed that Britain has been underinvesting since the Second World War. After that something will be said about the advantages to industry of a predictable and stable low inflation environment within which companies can plan, and on alternative approaches to reducing the low productivity tail of inefficient companies that still persists in so many industries.

Growth from 1979 to 1989

In the first 10 years of Mrs Thatcher's Government the conditions have been created for the renaissance of British industry—but this has not yet been achieved, for manufacturing output is still only 10 per cent above its 1979 level (Figure 1). In the 1980s manufacturing companies have been sub-contracting many activities, such as the maintenance and leasing of equipment, transport, communications and catering, to non-manufacturing companies, so the true growth of their output will exceed 10 per cent by a comfortable margin but most would still judge

**Figure 1:   Manufacturing Industries: Indices of Output,
Employment and Productivity**

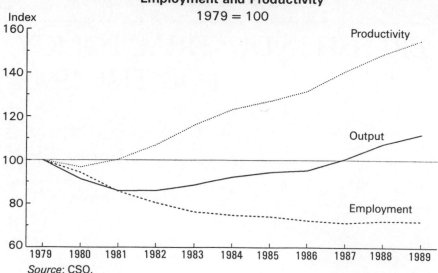

Source: CSO.

that the growth of United Kingdom manufacturing has not been
especially high.

There have, however, been favourable developments of great
importance: a 50 per cent advance in manufacturing productivity, a
more than doubling of the real rate of return on capital and at the same
time an increase of 30 per cent in real earnings per worker (Figure 2). It
is of course the 50 per cent rise in productivity that has provided the
wherewithal simultaneously to double the return on capital and raise
real wages by almost one-third. There is considerable controversy
about how this 50 per cent rise in productivity actually came about.
An important part of a plausible explanation is that the shock
administered to manufacturing industry from 1979 to 1982, when
output fell by 20 per cent, employment fell by one-third, and more
than 9,000 manufacturing companies became insolvent, placed immense pressures on the surviving firms to raise their productivity via a
reduction in unnecessary costs and a more effective use of labour and
capital if they were to avoid a similar fate. As a consequence,
managements went out of their way to achieve productivity increases
which had hitherto appeared unattainable, while unions and individual
employers agreed to new working arrangements which reduced
overmanning and increased flexibility in the deployment of labour.

Figure 2: Real Earnings and Real Rate of Return on Capital in Manufacturing

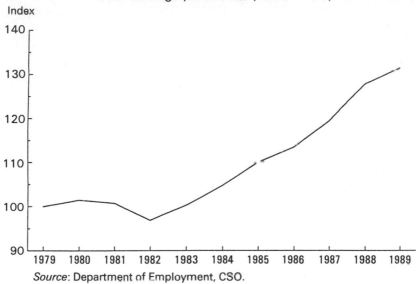

Real Earnings per Worker (1979 = 100)

Source: Department of Employment, CSO.

Real Rate of Return on Capital Employed

Source: Bank of England, DTI.

Figure 3: Investment in Manufacturing Industry: at Constant 1985 Prices

Source: CSO.

The reductions in marginal rates of taxation on corporate profits and on the personal incomes of managements that unfolded in the 1980s have been extremely helpful to the further advance of manufacturing productivity that continued after the crisis containment of the early 1980s. These factors, together with the scope for a considerable increase in real wages, created the conditions for positive-sum behaviour by both workers and managers who rapidly discovered that each could gain handsomely by co-operating to raise efficiency and to advance the international competitiveness of their products. The increase in productivity did not entail a very high rate of capital investment in manufacturing. This remained below the 1979 level until quite late in the decade and only began to exceed it in 1988 (Figure 3), but there was plausibly a very large improvement in the effectiveness with which capital was used. This occurred first because of the improvements in working arrangements that have been referred to and also because capital-augmenting technical progress has made it possible to buy more effective computer and IT equipment at a diminishing cost. Authors working in their own homes can purchase more effective personal computers at lower money prices than those of a decade ago and they have therefore been able to increase the effectiveness of their personal computers and at the same time invest a diminishing sum in this kind of equipment. A good deal of industry has been able to benefit in a similar manner because parallel technical developments have raised the effectiveness of machinery that utilises electronic and microchip programmes without a commensurate rise in what must be paid for it.

The United States has a quality-weighted price index for computer and IT equipment and this has been falling by more than 20 per cent a year relative to prices in general, so US firms have been able to obtain a 20 per cent enhancement of IT equipment per annum from a constant real rate of investment. There have been parallel developments in the UK. At the start of the new decade we therefore have the advantage of a more than 1979 level of investment together with a substantial increase in the productivity of capital which augurs well for the growth of productive capacity in the 1990s.

Weaknesses in the Product Range and Competitiveness

That is what has been achieved; what has not been achieved is a significant rise in the level of production, or an adequate level of competitiveness against imports in many sectors of manufacturing. It is extremely difficult to know how far the deterioration in trade performance in the later 1980s has been due to the macro-economic influence of an excessively rapid growth of demand in the UK and how much has been due to the narrowness of the range of products British industry can now manufacture, but all are agreed that there are weaknesses in the product range. This is true of a good deal of mechanical engineering and especially of machinery production where factory after factory is full of foreign machinery of types that British industry simply does not manufacture. The same is true of consumer electronic products. And in the vehicles industry it is controversial whether certain makes of British cars are less reliable than German and Japanese imports, but nowadays well over half the cars sold in Britain are imported.

It is plausible that the recovery of British industry had to pass through two stages. The first, where much progress has been made, involved the elimination of overmanning and of inefficient control over the use of economic resources. Achievements there have boosted real wages and profits and provided the wherewithal to embark on the vital second stage which we must now move on to. This will consist in the modernisation and development of the product range of much of UK industry so that the weaknesses I have referred to are gradually eliminated.

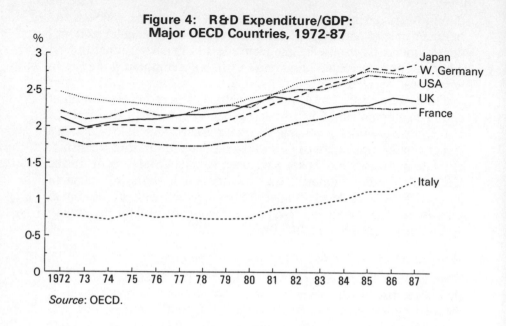

Figure 4:   R&D Expenditure/GDP:
Major OECD Countries, 1972-87

Source: OECD.

Figure 5:   R&D Expenditure Relative to GDP: Major OECD Countries, 1987

	R&D Expenditure			Government Funded R&D		
	Total R&D	Business R&D* Total	(Financed by business)	Total	Defence	Civil
	%	%	%	%	%	%
UK	2·3	1·5	(1·1)	1·1	0·5	0·6
France	2·3	1·4	(0·9)	1·4	0·5	0·9
West Germany	2·8	2·1	(1·8)	1·1	0·1	1·0
Italy	1·3	0·8	(0·5)	0·8	0·1	0·7
Japan	2·9	1·9	(1·9)	0·6	0·0	0·6
USA	2·7	1·9	(1·2)	1·3	0·9	0·4

*Including defence work

Source: OECD; Cabinet Office, *Annual Review of Government Funded Research and Development*, 1989.

Research and Development

From the economist's standpoint movements up market towards better products are achieved via improvements in design, research and development and in the whole process of innovation. With regard to research and development, UK expenditures (as a share of GDP) are lower than those of some of our leading competitors. In 1987 we spent 1·5 per cent of GDP on business research and development while West Germany, Japan and the United States spent around 2 per cent. But France spent about the same as we did and Italy considerably less and these countries have both been relatively successful in world markets (Figures 4 and 5). We should not, therefore, conclude that the expenditure of extra resources on research and development is all that is required. A change in managerial attitudes and organisation and the effectiveness with which knowledge is applied and exploited are also important.

What is especially heartening about prospects for the 1990s is that industry now has the money to expand research and development. Figure 6 shows an economist's approach—with the over-simplifications that this necessarily involves—to the incentive to companies to move up market. In the diagram a 'representative firm' can earn a rate of return of r if it makes no effort to move up market via research and development and improved designs and extra innovative expenditures of a general kind. Any extra expenditures to improve these will involve the establishment of enhanced research and development and sales divisions which will eat into company profitability in the short term but at the same time enable the firm to expand future sales. The schedule RR indicates how a willingness to sacrifice short-term profitability by building up research and other innovative expenditures will add to the growth of demand. If companies can obtain finance at a cost of i, they will be ready to finance extra growth obtained by these means until the marginal return from extra markets obtained is equal to the extra cost of finance required to buy them. In the diagram this is achieved at a rate of growth of g' at which the firm's rate of return on capital is r'. At a growth rate of g' the marginal return from expanded research and development, etc., just equals i, the cost of finance.

The incentive to move in this direction, that is, to expand research and development in order to achieve faster market growth, will be enhanced whenever r (the rate of profit) is raised, which will lift the RR schedule, or i (the cost of finance) is reduced. In Britain in the 1980s profit rates and interest rates have both risen sharply but the rise in

43

Figure 6: How High Profit Rates Create Scope for Innovative Expenditures

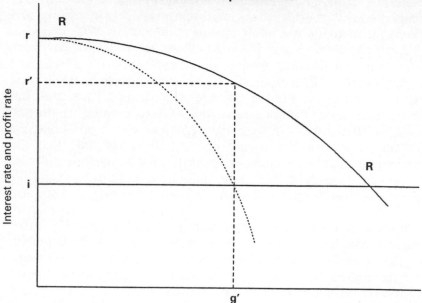

rate of growth of the market as a consequence
of innovative expenditures

profit rates has placed these significantly above even the present high level of interest rates (Figure 7). In consequence, there is currently an incentive to firms to finance moves up market in the manner that has been described. More generally, the excess of the rate of profit over the cost of finance means that there are clear incentives for UK firms to use internal and external finance to enhance their physical assets and the capital they devote to the creation of new processes and products.

Economic Climate for Innovation Essential

Following this approach, an essential element in government policy to aid research, development and innovation is to create an economic environment where companies have financial room to develop new products and processes. This requires above all policies which will, in the medium term, lead to higher rates of return on capital, especially after tax, and at the same time exert a downward pressure on interest rates and therefore the cost of finance.

Figure 7: Real Rates of Return on Capital Employed and Real Rates of Interest

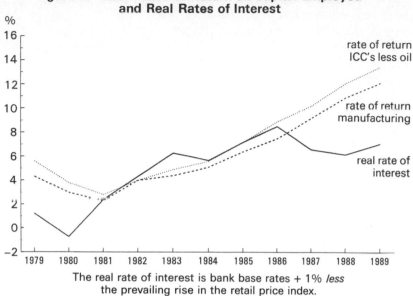

The real rate of interest is bank base rates + 1% *less* the prevailing rise in the retail price index.

Source: CSO, Bank of England, DTI (updated NEDO estimates).

In general, real interest rates tend to be quite similar in the world's leading economies because of the ease of international arbitrage in bill and bond markets, but the return on capital can differ considerably because there are not equally clear arbitrage opportunities in international equity markets. In the 1960s and the 1970s German and Japanese companies earned far higher rates of return on capital than UK companies while all paid much the same real interest rates. It followed that the resources and incentives available to German and Japanese companies to finance extra expenditures on research and development were that much greater, and it is not surprising that in many industries their producers were therefore able to move up market in relation to UK producers, which led to a continual weakening of the competitiveness of British against German and Japanese producers in home and world markets. In the first 10 years of Mrs Thatcher's Government the real rate of return on capital has been raised to a level that is far closer to real rates of return in Japanese and German industry, and after the long time-lags associated with such developments, it is to be hoped that research and development into superior products and processes will respond to the enhanced

45

incentives to invest in innovative activity that this should bring about. It is heartening that, at the start of 1990, the CBI reported that, despite 15 per cent base rates, 40 per cent of UK companies are planning to expand their spending on innovative activity and only 10 per cent to cut it.

Some would still see research and development policy as involving detailed intervention by the state to throw money at potential winners and it is widely believed that the French and Japanese (but not the Germans) have benefited in the past from policies of this kind. This may or may not have been the case but it is only too clear that UK efforts to pick winners have been extraordinarily unsuccessful. In the early 1950s we spent as much as 3 per cent of our national income on the nuclear energy programme which at that time provided something like 3 per cent of our electricity [Maddock (1975)] and where the long-term benefits its proponents expected have up to now eluded us. Only one UK-designed reactor has so far been exported after 40 years of nuclear research. Concorde has also proved extremely expensive and unexportable, and it is only flown by the airlines of the two countries which developed it. Because of such dreadful examples it is unlikely that many will wish to encourage future British governments to attempt to pick winners in the research and development area. The government does, of course, finance a good deal of military research and development (it has been greatly to the advantage of the Germans and Japanese that they have been largely precluded from this), and it will be worthwhile in view of the thaw in East-West relations to examine how far military research can be guided further towards projects which also have important civil applications in the world's export markets. With that said, the essence of research and development policy must be to develop the economy in a manner which will have a general tendency to raise net-of-tax rates of return on capital and to reduce the long-term level of real interest rates, in order to provide financial scope for companies to use more extensive internal and borrowed financial resources to enhance product designs and research and development.

Skill Shortages

Another area of weakness in British industry which has been widely recognised is a comparative lack of skills and education of the labour force. Comparative data on education and training need to be used with caution, but particularly at further education level, participation rates in Britain are significantly lower than in the major overseas economies. Participation in full-time education by 16- and 17-year-olds, for example, is at around 90 per cent in Japan and the USA but significantly lower in Britain at just under 50 per cent and just over 30 per cent for 16- and 17-year-olds respectively. The least educated third of the labour force is particularly unqualified in comparison with most of our leading overseas competitors [Department of Employment (1989)].

The precise relationship between vocational education and training and competitiveness is difficult to establish, but detailed comparative micro studies in selected manufacturing and service industries conducted by the National Institute of Economic and Social Research during the 1980s suggest that the link is a strong one. Comparing several US and UK manufacturing industries, for example, Daly (1984) found that the upgrading of 1 per cent of the labour force from the unskilled to the skilled category raised productivity by about 2 per cent. Research by Worswick (1985) has shown that lower-skilled workforces require more overhead labour in the form of quality controllers and production planners. Other research has shown that the strength of a broadly-trained and retrained intermediate skill-base in West German mechanical engineering firms has helped companies to cope with changing competence requirements in that sector. This has not been possible to anything like the same extent in Britain [Campbell, Sorge and Warner (1989)].

Adjusting to the moving skills target is a corporate problem but it has a national dimension. Almost without exception competitors from abroad see education and training as a vital element in competitiveness. The French are aiming for 75 per cent of their young people to reach undergraduate entry level by the end of the century [CBI (1989)]. Those countries which aim to climb the industrial league table also see education as a key element in the process of transformation. The South Koreans are reported to be aiming to have 80 per cent of their young people reach university entrance standard by the end of the century. In this country the Secretary of State for Employment has suggested that by the year 2000 a minimum of half the employed workforce should be qualified to level three National Vocational Qualification or its academic equivalent (in England GCE 'A' level) [Norman Fowler (1989)]. At present about 30 per cent of young people achieve this level. Attaining this target would represent a significant improvement on what has been achieved so far, but reaching it would not move us alongside the leaders.

The skills of the labour force depend very much on the training policies of companies and it is important to note that a number of new factors are beginning to have a favourable influence on employer training decisions. The reduction in numbers of school leavers which will continue in the early 1990s is already causing good employers to consider the recruitment of older workers and the retraining and upgrading of their existing workforces. It is now widely accepted that, for the future, young people leaving school should be encouraged not to enter employment without training. Public funding for training credits for young people and better careers advice, as suggested by the CBI in its report, *Towards A Skills Revolution* (1989), would underpin this important advance. The Single European Market is focussing employers' minds on competitiveness. These factors provide a unique opportunity to change attitudes and to influence employer decisions.

Government training schemes, largely operated through the Training Agency and its predecessor bodies have, if anything, remained more distant from the development of 'the skills industry needs'. The Youth Training Scheme, Employment Training and other schemes have been designed to attempt to avoid financial support by the Government for training which it saw as the responsibility of employers. Objectives were not always realised in practice and the Youth Training Scheme, for instance, which was intended to augment employer expenditure, has actually resulted in a considerable substitution of government expenditure for employer expenditure on youth training.

Private Funding of Training Must Be Augmented

There is a serious danger that private funding for training will not generate a level of spending which is consistent with a substantial change in the relative performance of the British economy. There are two major reasons for this. The first is the scale of change required. A serious backlog of educational and training under-achievement has accumulated over a long period and competitor countries are stepping up their commitment to training. Second, there is an apparent lack of belief among many employers and employees in the value of education and training. At the same time, many employers who would accept the existence of a link between training expenditure and competitiveness are inhibited from effective action by fears of poaching. This is common because skilled labour is in such short supply, and employers who are not confident of their ability to retain staff will not expect to enjoy the full value of their investments in training.

There are therefore strong arguments for government to cut directly into the training system, by augmenting employers' spending. The extension of the 'training credit' idea to embrace older workers and not just the 16-18 year-olds could be considered. More positively, individual training credits could provide a substantial new 'cultural' pressure within the economy. There are many practical considerations which need to be thought through before firm proposals can be made, but in principle there is much to commend this line of policy.

A practical approach to such a credit system for young people is set out in the CBI Vocational Education and Training Task Force led by Sir Bryan Nicholson in *Towards a Skills Revolution*. For adults there might similarly need to be a requirement for an Individual Action Plan agreed with the employer. Whether it would be possible to stipulate that such plans should form a part of a thorough-going training plan, or whether higher-value credits might be available in such circumstances, could be explored. Certainly government funding for the derivation of such plans under the Business Growth Training Scheme needs to be sustained and possibly expanded.

A financial credit which would be offered to all in the relevant age group could entitle the employee to a part of or the whole of a full- or part-time course of education or a course of training provided by an Approved Training Organisation. For some individuals this could provide an opportunity to obtain a recognised qualification, perhaps taking advantage of an assessed allowance for experience and previous training undergone. In other cases the credit would allow a higher qualification to be attained. Although there are strong arguments for a flat-rate scheme, the reasons for differential funding, with more for those in some occupational groups where training costs are necessarily higher, ought to be explored. Those individuals who can justify leaving their jobs to undertake a full-time course of study would, as under existing funding arrangements, require a maintenance grant as well as the covering of course fees. It has to be said that there is no way in which it could be ensured that training credits would not result in some substitution of public for employer expenditure. But making the payments individually based should help. This would increase the opportunities open to individuals and give them greater economic leverage when decisions on training are taken. The less effective employers might not be able to take advantage of the facility but with a

Training and Enterprise Council's help their employees should benefit. The effective employers would as a result of the credit system have even more competent employees, who would earn more, pay more taxes and should (the acid test of the scheme) cover the cost to the government of the training over a period.

These proposals are put forward tentatively. There is a strong case for a substantial increase in expenditure on education and training. There is an even stronger case that such expenditures should be focussed on improvements in competitiveness. But it is difficult to see the gap being fully covered by private employers without some kind of financial assistance from government. It is to be noted that the suggested policy development discussed above has a good deal in common with the educational voucher schemes which some have wished to introduce to increase the responsiveness of schools to educational needs as perceived by pupils and parents. In a parallel manner, training vouchers should help to steer job training towards the perceived needs of workers who wish to enhance their skills, which should in turn increase the sensitivity of training to the actual economic requirements of British industry and commerce.

Fiscal Incentives

Many would wish to reinforce industrial policy by subsidising capital investment, research and development and training through the tax system. Company expenditures on research, development and training can already be written off in effect at rates of 100 per cent, while capital investment can be depreciated faster in general than the rate at which capital becomes obsolete. Twenty-five per cent of the nominal value of investment can be written off each year at a reducing-balance rate which means that, so long as inflation is less than 10 per cent, at least 15 per cent of the real value of investments can be written off against tax each year, which is more than adequate to cover the effective capital lives of 10 years or more in most industries. A faster rate of permitted write-off would involve what is in effect a tax subsidy. In the case of certain kinds of IT equipment where economic lives are shorter, faster write-offs against tax are already permitted.

The question for government is whether it is preferable to assist industry by lowering the rate of Corporation Tax to the greatest degree possible and to refrain from subsidising capital investment, research and development and training through the tax system, or whether it is preferable that companies should pay lower effective taxation only in so far as they push their spending in these directions. Mrs Thatcher's Government has moved towards a lower overall rate of corporation tax, and the removal of what are regarded as investment subsidies. This has had the advantage of reducing distortions (Australia now allows Research and Development expenditures to be written off at 150 per cent and this creates strong incentives to companies to class as wide a range of activities as possible as Research and Development), but it is likely that it has also led to a lower aggregate level of expenditure on capital investment. It is a matter of judgement whether the gains in the quality of investment have been more important than any adverse effects on its quantity. There is no doubt, however, that the achievement of a 35 per cent Corporation Tax rate—the lowest of any major member of the European Community—has been of great benefit to industry, and a powerful attraction to overseas companies to locate in the UK.

The Advantages to Industry from Low Inflation

There is another element of government policy which is extremely important to industry and that is the achievement of a low and stable rate of inflation. This is most important in relation to the predictability and stability of government policy which is vital to industry and which can be delivered only when inflation is at an acceptably low rate. If, as in 1989, inflation rises to a rate which is regarded as unacceptably high and that is higher than in the other leading members of the European Community, all are aware that there will be future policy shifts to bring inflation back to an acceptable level. Whether these will take the form of a temporary period of abnormally high interest rates or an un-competitive exchange rate or of higher future taxation or the cancellation of government-funded investment projects will be unclear to business, but all will be aware that some of these are in the offing whenever inflation takes off. This is extremely damaging to the ability of companies to plan ahead and German and Japanese industrialists have not had to face the same degree of dislocation from government-induced stop-go cycles as British and United States producers have suffered from. It is weaknesses in the control of inflation in these countries followed by deflationary periods to bring it down again that have been responsible for much of the stop-go.

In the UK the 1980s offered stable inflation at an acceptable rate from 1983 to 1988, which was a great improvement on the 1960s and the 1970s, but the acceleration of inflation in 1989—and it will continue at an unacceptably high rate in 1990—has again introduced a margin of uncertainty about the impact of deflationary government policies which is bound to be unfavourable to companies. A greater degree of success in macro-economic policies to place sustained downward pressure on inflation (which is an especial concern of other contributors to this conference) is therefore also of great importance to the ability of manufacturing companies to plan ahead.

There is also a technical argument concerning the benefits to industry from a low rate of inflation which is not widely understood. The incentive to companies to invest and to spend on research and development in order to move up market depends considerably, as was argued above, on the excess of the rate of return on capital over the rate of interest, because it is this that enables companies to take advantage of external finance which enormously enhances the potential growth rate of those with particular prospects for the launch of successful products. Superficially a faster rate of inflation should raise the nominal rate of return on capital and nominal interest rates about equally and so leave the balance between prospective profits and interest largely unchanged; but it does not have a neutral impact in practice. It is misleading to suppose that five percentage points on inflation will raise both the prospective return on capital and nominal interest rates by 5 per cent. One reason has already been referred to. If the business community believes that a five percentage point increase in inflation will at some point be corrected via future deflationary policy, prospective profit rates will not rise by five percentage points because companies will not anticipate that they will be allowed to earn the extra profits—if they believe that profit margins will be squeezed.

Rising Inflation Squeezes Profits

But there is a further important difference in the impact of faster inflation on profit rates and interest rates. Interest contracts are not indexed against inflation so when inflation increases by 5 per cent the short-term interest rates companies have to pay will generally rise by around five percentage points. But company profits are not raised at all in the short term by an increase in inflation. If anything, company costs tend to increase a little faster than prices when inflation rises, so profit margins are slightly squeezed. The compensation for a 5 per cent increase in inflation to companies takes the form of a tendency for future profits to be raised by inflation at an extra compound rate of 5 per cent, as prices and wages and other costs all increase at a cumulative annual rate of 5 per cent.

So faster inflation will have a general tendency to raise immediate interest payments far more than immediate profits with the result that the ratio of interest payments to profits will increase quite sharply. This will lead to the financial failure of companies that are at all vulnerable, and it has been estimated that each 1 per cent rise in the rate of inflation has tended to increase the number of bankruptcies in the UK by 5·8 per cent [Wadhwani (1984)].

Because faster inflation has this asymmetrical impact on nominal profits and interest, it undermines the incentive to borrow by all who are uncertain about the future, and it shatters the finances of those who have borrowed heavily in the past on terms where interest rates can be adjusted upwards by lenders, as is the case with all bank borrowing. These embarrassments are now affecting all in the UK who have borrowed from banks or building societies, and are paying three or four percentage points more than they expected when they took out their loans.

If this analysis is correct, then the main boon that the government could offer to industry in the 1990s would be an environment where inflation is at a low and predictably steady rate, and where nominal interest rates therefore become considerably lower than they are at the start of the decade. At the same time it is vital that workers and companies should both continue to benefit from economic growth so that the incentive to co-operate which we have benefited from so much since 1983 can continue. German and Japanese industry has benefited from conditions where economic growth boosted both wages and profits in a manner where workers and industrialists both learned that they stood to gain far more from continuous production than from conflicts to distribute the gains more in favour of either wages or profits. It is vital that the conditions for such co-operation are sustained.

The Need to Transform British Industry's Low Productivity Tail

A final element of industrial policy that deserves emphasis is the transformation of the tail of weak companies that still persists in many areas of UK industry with relatively low productivity, low wages and skills and unreliable quality standards. Competition will in due course eliminate this tail, but inefficient companies that pay badly and have not borrowed significantly can survive for one or two decades. Their ultimate failure will have enormous economic and social costs that can devastate communities, whilst in the meantime a proportion of the nation's economic resources is being inefficiently used. The ideal solution is to use the period before failure is inevitable to transform as many such companies as possible. One way in which this is coming about is through the high quality standards that effectively managed corporations can impose on the weaker companies in their supply chain. One very successful Japanese-owned machine-tool firm in the Midlands buys components and parts from a larger number of UK suppliers than it employs workers. Where high standards are insisted on by final manufacturers there can be a favourable impact on hundreds of other producers in their supply chain. The major companies which have raised their own standards in the 1980s should thus help others to do the same in the 1990s.

The second approach to transforming the tail is to obtain and convey information to the managements of the weaker companies about best practice. This has a dynamic aspect as well. Many companies which are presently strong, or at least adequate, can all too readily be 'caught out' by a world which changes at a much faster pace in every dimension from markets to processes. The need to help them to shed outmoded strategies has never been greater.

If there was a perfect supply of correct information this would be superfluous, but Britain's industrial history in the last 80 years demonstrates how readily the inefficient can co-exist with other superbly performing companies. Rational managers do not ignore evidence about the behaviour of their competitors and peers, as evidenced by the popularity of various management techniques and books—such as John Humble, *Management by Objectives* (1972), and Thomas Peters and Robert Waterman, *In Search of Excellence: Lessons from America's Best Run Companies* (1982). But it is easy for observers to underestimate the difficulty of obtaining information that is sufficiently specific to a sector or to a particular kind of company for a practising manager to draw practical conclusions with confidence. It is easy to underestimate the demands of running a company—not least one that is underperforming. Hence, to be useful, information on best practice has to be specific, readily assimilable and delivered in a manner which captures the attention of the busy manager.

The NEDC's Role in Correcting Inefficient Underperformance

The role of ascertaining the facts about why and to what extent the inefficient underperform and the determination of what corrective action is needed is the principal task of the National Economic Development Council's industrial Sector Groups. Committees with a strong representation of effective managements, and trade unions and the government are ideally constituted to establish the facts on best practice, to identify areas of weakness, to suggest the best practical ways of correcting them and to initiate programmes to communicate these effectively to companies.

The participation of very senior industrialists in these committees— and many chairmen and managing directors of major companies are members—ensures that any recommendations about best practice will have high credibility. The participation of senior trade unionists as well as representatives of government means that the recommendations that emerge will be acknowledged to be free of partisanship so that they can be regarded as a move to enhance performance from which all should benefit.

At present the National Economic Development Council's Committees and Working Parties cover about half of manufacturing industry including most but not all of the sectors in which there are demonstrably correctable performance deficiencies. This approach to improving industrial performance could be more effective if the committees were able to monitor the whole of UK industry in a systematic manner in order to identify the greatest opportunities to improve performance.

The impartial analysis thus obtained would be valuable to managers in the manner I have described and would also be of value to government in determining the impact of its own measures. Indeed, the combination of such a process of independent industrial assessment with the steps to improve the operating environment for industry, which are outlined in the earlier part of the paper, provide a general basis for the continuing improvement of the performance of UK industry.

REFERENCES

Campbell, Adrian, Arnte Sorge and Malcolm Warner (1989): *Microelectronics, Product Applications in Great Britain and West Germany*, Gower.

Confederation of British Industry (1989): *Towards a Skills Revolution*, London: CBI.

Daly, Anne (1984): *Education, Training and Productivity in the US and GB*, Discussion Paper No. 63, London: NIESR.

Department of Employment (1989): *Training in Britain: a Study of Funding Activity and Attitudes* (The Main Report), London: HMSO.

Fowler, Norman (1989): Secretary of State for Employment, *Speech to 'Business in the Cities Conference'*, 6 December.

Humble, John (1972): *Management by Objectives*, British Institute of Management.

Maddock, Sir Ieuan (1975): 'Science, Technology and Industry', in *Proceedings of the Royal Society of London*, (Series A), Vol. 345, pp. 295-326.

Peters, Thomas J. and Robert H. Waterman (1982): *In Search of Excellence: Lessons from America's Best-Run Companies*, New York: Harper and Row.

Wadhwani, Sushil B. (1984): 'Inflation, bankruptcy, default premia and the stock market', Discussion Paper No. 194, Centre for Labour Economics, London School of Economics.

Worswick, David (1985): *Education and Economic Performance*, Gower.

4

THE BRITISH ECONOMY AND CURRENT WEAKNESSES

David Lomax
National Westminster Bank

Introduction

AS WE MOVE INTO the 1990s the UK economy is in financial disequilibrium, with the rate of inflation too high and the balance-of-payments in serious deficit. This situation has stemmed from the excess consumer demand in 1988, in turn financed largely by the housing boom of that year, which in turn was related to the lax credit policies pursued for too long.

Looking to the longer term, the UK has too small an export sector, which means that the supply-side effects of the last 10 years have not yet achieved the capacity required. Britain has too few major companies dominating top industries. Growth is likely to be held back by balance-of-payments constraints.

Industry

The UK has few home-grown companies with strong or dominant positions in the major industries, such as motors, electronics, telecommunications, trucks and aerospace, for example. Many of our companies have recently come under foreign ownership. This increases the risk of UK capacity being treated as branch plants as companies rationalise for the future.

We still have examples of trade unions obstructing the creation of efficient capacity in the UK, such as in the automobile industry, when it is transparently obvious that there are alternative sites abroad, and that only efficient capacity will survive.

Many of the supply-side innovations over the past decade have been extremely sensible and very valuable. The benefits to the UK have, however, to be set against strong competitive forces operating in the other direction.

Some countries have been doing the same thing, consciously and deliberately, like France. Other countries have extremely efficient companies which have pressed on regardless with stunning strength, like Germany.

Rationalisation in some industries has been taking place world-wide, and Europe-wide in others, as the 1980s started with excess capacity. Because of their size or structure of ownership many UK-based plants were not particularly well placed to face that situation.

New international competition has been felt in many markets, especially from Japan. Britain started the decade with a small industrial base, and we have not been able to transform that situation. Indeed the recession of the early 1980s knocked out some good capacity.

The game of re-organising European industry through mergers and acquisitions is being played with considerable skill and determination by some countries, notably France, and with considerable commercial strength by others, notably Germany. This will cramp the room for manoeuvre of British companies.

In industries such as banking, strength goes to a large extent with capital weight, which in turn relates to the strength of the currency and the size of the economies in which banks are located. Increasing competitive pressure, stemming from events such as Big Bang of 1986 and the liberalisation within Europe for the Single Market in 1992, means that the banks with spare capacity, from the strongest economies, can extend their ownership and competitive pressure elsewhere throughout the Community.

I am not concerned to argue that the British manufacturing sector must be of a certain size, nor that we should go to state corporatism. Nevertheless, these factors do not make it easier to achieve our desired economic growth, based on exponential expansion from our current base. What is required in order to improve this situation?

The Supply-Side

The recent supply-side policy has been the right one. The only successful policy must be to continue with it. We cannot create major companies overnight. We therefore have to create an enterprise economy and hope that enough seeds will grow to produce the increased capacity we need in many areas of industry and commerce. In most areas of policy the fundamentals of the enterprise economy, in terms of the availability of finance, incentives, and other resources, seem adequate, and I have no comments on those. As one goes through life one learns that if you do something silly it is amazing how disastrous the result may be, while if you behave sensibly it is often equally amazing how cumulative the benefits become. In the situation in which we find ourselves the UK has no choice but to be sensible and efficient, creating the ground rules for enterprise. It then has to wait to see enterprises created through the investment of capital to supply potential markets.

There are areas where management appears to be somewhat weak in the face of still powerful unions, such as perhaps in some parts of public transport. There are other areas where unions seem determined to commit economic suicide once they have any power. But there seems no need for any particular change in legislation. In most areas of the economy management can manage, which in turn is a condition for future higher real incomes for all.

Education and Training

There is one supply-side area where the present government's performance has been execrable. This relates to education and training. It is by now standard market economics that certain goods and services may be underprovided if supply is left entirely to market forces. These are the goods and services which are linked with externalities or are public goods, or where income deficiencies may prevent there being adequate demand for the goods or services in question. It is entirely right that many economists nowadays should examine much more closely the issue of externalities and public goods, to see whether property rights may be created which could bring the provision of those goods and services more within the private domain. Nevertheless, until solutions have been found to those problems of redefinition of rights, the adequate supply of those goods and services will require public support, through public spending or public support for private arrangements. It is the charlatan's version of market economics to argue that such goods and services should be provided only to the extent to which the private sector is willing to pay for them. A key area where public support is required is training and education.

If the UK wishes to succeed in a competitive world, as a high income country, then it has to move up market in quality and skills. Cheap people producing cheap products only generate cheap incomes. The way to prosperity is to supply quality products and to obtain a higher price for them—a policy at which Germany is a master. Our supply-side policies must be geared to quality at all levels.

It has been obvious for many years, certainly well beyond a decade, that the standard of school-leaving education and of vocational training in the UK has been appalling. There has been a substantial sum spent on training, but much of the original impetus was related to helping the unemployed youth deal with short-term problems. The recent initiative regarding Training and Enterprise Councils and the CBI initiative are steps in the right direction. But far more is required. It is time we had an establishment consensus that we need to improve massively the quality of the training offered to young people joining the workforce and to people who wish to re-skill themselves. Here the failure of this Government is particularly disappointing since what they have actually done flies in the face of their ostensible objectives of improving the supply side of the economy and of providing young people with greater opportunities.

Regional Prosperity

If training is an area where the Government is faced with serious problems and needs to pull its socks up, regional policy in contrast is at present in a state which could hardly be better for the Government. It is almost a perfect situation for government policy-makers. A favourable trend is on the way. All the Government has to do is to acknowledge it, give it a helping hand, and then claim the political benefits. This Government faces enormous opportunities at relatively little cost. For decades we have been concerned with the problems of the older industrial areas, with their high unemployment and their low income levels. It was impossible to make people leave London. A series of regional policies was introduced, including licensing control for office and factory development, with the intention of holding down the South East and encouraging the rest. I am glad to say that one of the first acts of this present Government was to abolish those controls.

What do we see now? Many provincial areas are booming. The property market is far healthier in many provincial towns than it is in London and the South East. People are keen to leave London. Several government departments and many commercial organisations have moved out of London to Bristol and beyond in the West, to the Midlands, to the North West, to East Anglia and to the North. One hears few complaints. Looking to the future, the property investment potential in the provinces seems far stronger than in the South East. What are the reasons for this change, and are they likely to persist?

Real Incomes in an Integrated Economy—the UK's Geographic Advantage

Economic theory would lead us to expect an equalisation of real incomes over areas which are economically integrated. If users of resources have the option of choosing between different locations they will tend to choose the one which is the most profitable or which gives the best value for money. There are certain cumulative or hysteresis effects which may benefit some locations, and we must not forget transport costs, but in general one would expect not to see major anomalies in real incomes between areas which are integrated economically.

A key reason for the closer integration of the UK, with people able to carry out their jobs efficiently in many areas of the country, is the improved infrastructure in terms of telecommunications, roads and railways. The economic distance between what we have long regarded as fairly distant parts of the UK has been much reduced, in terms of immediacy of communications, time for travel, and cost of transport. The UK is less than half the size of France, England is about a quarter the size of France, and the core of the English population between, say, Bristol, Lancashire, Yorkshire and London, live in an area smaller than Maine. What we have tended to regard as different regions, such as London, the West Midlands and the East Midlands, would be regarded by people in other parts of the world as simply slightly distant suburbs. Once the basic infrastructure was put in place the true geography of the UK could show itself. Markets could be integrated up and down the country.

The core prosperity, the extended London area, now reaches beyond Bristol to the West, and through the Midlands well into Lancashire and Yorkshire. Northern Ireland is a special case. Scotland is obviously furthest away from the South East, but has been showing signs of relative prosperity. Perhaps the most difficult of the English regions is the North East but even this is showing some benefits, and has been the recipient of substantial Japanese investment.

The fundamental force behind companies wishing to move from the South East has been the sharp difference in regional nominal costs, as the property boom of the 1980s hit the South East first and hit it hard. For the first time both companies and their staff wished to leave the South East. The companies wanted to do so because it was cheaper, and the staff because they could buy far better accommodation in the regions. It is this development, with both companies and staff wishing to leave London, which has been the crucial change. House prices are now falling in the South East, so the price gradient may change. Nevertheless, one would expect prices to remain significantly higher in the South East than elsewhere, and for this gradient to persist. Once one has broken through the psychological barrier then the fundamental forces pushing people and companies away from London are likely to be maintained.

Ricardo, Hirsch and Wealth-related Scarce Goods

I have a theory for the increase in the price gradient for property assets between London and the provinces, which I will now test run here. This relates to the accumulation of wealth through the ages and the impact of Ricardo's theory of rent on relative asset prices. Asset values are destroyed in wars and recessions. We have had neither of these for over 40 years. Wealth has steadily accumulated. Taking into account Ricardo's theory of rent, and Fred Hirsch's application of it to consumption, the implication of this is that the prices of the scarcest goods rise systematically. The price of the scarcest good of all, say a van Gogh, rises to match the wealth of the richest person who wishes to bid for it. In other words, the price of a van Gogh is wealth related and not income related. The same thing clearly applies to other scarce goods, such as the scarcest property (and perhaps the scarcest golf courses). Thus one would expect the prices of top real estate around the world, say in New York, Paris and London, to rise with this steady, persistent accumulation of wealth. In due course we should expect to see core areas of scarcity, such as the centre of London, where prices would be wealth related and not linked to what people can afford to pay out of their earnings.

When I have put this theory forward in the past people have said to me: 'Well, what is different? What's new?' What is new is that this process of wealth accumulation has gone on now for over 40 years in the longest and strongest boom in world history, at a time of relatively great population density. Before the First World War this theory would show itself only in small areas, given the levels of population and wealth. Economic and military events since then led to no major appreciation of asset values until after 1945.

As a result of this, one would expect property values in the scarce areas to become increasingly out of reach of those buying from earnings. Such people would be forced to move away from those areas. This is precisely what has happened, with it being virtually impossible to get into the housing market in London at less than £60,000. That figure is out of reach of many young people starting off in their careers. This process is thus catapulting young people away from London. An additional factor is that the UK, and indeed Western Europe as a whole, is an area of relatively stable population. There will be a shortage of young people in the UK over the coming years. Thus I envisage a situation where the young people will flee London so as to be able to find accommodation, and companies will pursue them with vigour into any area where there is a trained labour force. This spread effect from London should be very marked in the early 1990s.

Thus the conclusion is that this Government, and indeed any government, is within striking distance of announcing an end to the regional problems of the UK as we have known them, and of taking the credit for a massive relative improvement in the prosperity of the provinces. If the Government is going to be criticised for the uniform business rate it may as well take the credit for the prosperity being generated in the regions. Tighter planning controls in the South East have the twin political benefits of pleasing those living in the South East and of driving people and their employers to the provinces. This process of integration throughout the UK is now well underway and does not require excessive special action by the Government. The process will clearly be helped if local government in the regions adopts sensible policies which encourage economic activity. The Government should do as little as it can which would have the effect of thwarting this process. There is one area where positive action may be required, and from which the Government should also be able to take further credit. This relates to the role of infrastructure spending.

Infrastructure Spending

One cynical view about ideas for infrastructure spending is that the construction industry is trying simply to find a means of obtaining money to keep itself busy. One should never completely rule out cynicism, but that is not fundamentally a relevant point.

A second argument for infrastructure spending is that put forward cogently by the CBI recently, relating to the cost of congestion and the adverse effect on business efficiency. It is not easy to calculate the optimum way of using limited resources to ease congestion and maximise growth. These cost-benefit calculations need to be treated with something of a pinch of salt. Nevertheless, the fundamental argument of the CBI is sound and if there are excessive costs caused by inefficient infrastructure, then money should be spent to remove the blockages.

An argument has been put forward in government, particularly within the present administration, that the private sector, under market forces, should pay for such infrastructure requirements. I have no quarrel with the way in which the present administration has stirred the argument, and put pressure on participants in the communications business to become more efficient and find new ways of financing investments. The deregulation of British telecommunications has been a force in helping the economic integration of the UK through cheaper telecommunications. Beneficiaries from planning gain, such as in Docklands, have been expected to contribute to road costs. But having achieved benefits, by expecting companies to be more careful about infrastructure spending, and to find new ways of financing it, that is a policy which becomes an abomination if taken too far. To argue from the Channel Tunnel or from Docklands that only the infrastructure should be built which can be financed by the private sector is a complete travesty of market economics. In areas where there are externalities or public goods, there may be a decisive role for the public sector to play.

The Single UK Market

What seems to me to be by far the strongest argument for the infrastructure expenditure necessary to reap the full benefits of this regional transformation of the UK is the concept of the Single Market. This Government wishes to see a Single European Market. *A fortiori*, it wishes to see a Single UK Market. The achievement of the qualities of a single market was one of the reasons behind the regional spread of prosperity in recent years. For two areas to be part of a single market it is necessary that the 'economic distance' between them should be negligible or small. This means that factors of production should be mobile between them, cost of movement of goods and services between them should be small or negligible, and prices should be free to adjust to offset any difference in real rewards necessitated by geographic factors. In practical terms this means that the telecommunications structure should be efficient and of adequate capacity. It also requires that the physical transport of people and goods should be through efficient means, such as modern railways and motor networks, and without congestion. Once those phenomena are in place economic forces can effectively have their way in determining the allocation of resources. What, of course, we see in the UK is in many cases higher nominal incomes and asset values in the South East but higher real incomes elsewhere in the country.

Creating a single market thus requires economic action by the government, mainly in the form of any necessary deregulation and public spending. But, fundamentally, the desire to create a Single UK Market as part of a Single European Market is a political objective. The justification for government action is as much political as economic.

Without wishing to carry the argument to extremes, and to have dual carriageways built to the door of every cottage, if the Government wishes to see the political objective of a single market, then the political ends have to will the means. In other words, as with any other political objective, there may well be economic arguments for determining how it is achieved, but fundamentally the end wills the means. The means of achieving an efficient single market in the UK need to be put in place. I can make this point with a clear conscience, not convicting myself of being a fiscal extravagant, because the UK benefits from its geography, so that the cost of putting in efficient infrastructure should be far less than in many other countries. We have nothing like the geographic distance to contend with as do many other countries. Whatever the quality of modern infrastructure which is required, it should cost significantly less in the UK *per capita* than in many other countries.

Strengthen Road and Rail Networks ex. London

There clearly will be a need for much greater investment in London itself, but preferably in railways and tubes. The difficulty of putting roads in heavily congested areas is that they cost a fortune, they take ages to build, they create enormous local environmental problems, and they fill up with cars straight away, moving at the previous rate of about 12 miles an hour. Thus there is a substantial argument for using the available money to spread activity away from London. In my view this would mean having a cross-Thames link as far down the Thames as possible, to take the Channel traffic to the north and east of London. One would then strengthen the national road and rail networks so as to enable activity to spread as far as possible throughout the UK. Transport links between the Continent and all areas of the UK should be improved, and may need to be deregulated further. The abolition of the National Dock Labour Scheme was a step in the right direction. The cost of the extra provincial roads would be virtually trivial because of the relatively small lengths of extra route required, and the fact that expenditure is bound to be spread over many years. The entire rail network should be brought up to modern standards as rapidly as possible, and in my view it is unacceptable for modernising investment to be held back by any external financing limits (EFL).

At present the regeneration of the provinces in the UK is proceeding at a pace which is taking many people by surprise, including people in the regions. The reasons for this are in my view extremely clear. Some should be credited to the present administration, while others relate to actions by previous governments or to forces which are outside governmental control. Market forces are pushing very strongly in the desired direction, but they will need and should receive some support from the Government. We should thus reasonably hope to see the UK regional situation transformed by the early-1990s through the proper use of precisely the market forces which this Government believes to be so constructive.

Summary and Conclusions

1. In the short term the UK suffers from excess inflationary pressure, which is being redressed by current policies.

2. Britain has too weak an industrial sector. The benefits from supply-side policies come up against similar policies pursued by other countries. The world-wide competitive environment is not helpful to the relative expansion of British industry.

3. The present supply-side policies are broadly speaking the correct ones and they should be continued.

4. An area where the present Government's policies have been particularly disappointing relates to education and training. It has been transparently obvious for many years that the levels of school-leaving education and of vocational training have in the UK been woeful in comparison with other countries. High incomes require trained people producing quality products. The Government's commitment to education and training should be massively enhanced.

5. In the area of regional development in the UK, the trends are heavily in the Government's favour. Companies and staff both wish to move away from the South East. Because of past investment in infrastructure, telecommunications, railways and roads, the UK is now much more integrated economically. Once it became possible to function efficiently away from the South East, companies and staff have been keen to take advantage of price and cost differentials.

6. The accumulation of wealth over the past 45 years has led to sharp increases in asset values in areas of the greatest scarcity, such as central London, which has put property out of the reach of people buying from earnings. The 1990s will show a shortage of young people nationwide, and companies will be seeking out trained staff throughout the country. The spread of prosperity from London should be very strong over those years.

7. The Government should take action to further this process, by the necessary infrastructure spending to create a Single UK Market. The main investment in London should be in various forms of railways. Channel traffic should be taken north and east of London. Provincial communications should be improved to the necessary quality. In view of the UK's very small geographic size, the cost of achieving any desired quality of infrastructure in the UK is likely to be much lower *per capita* than in many other industrial countries.

8. There is an essential role for government in ensuring the provision of goods and services which are public goods, which lead to substantial externalities, or which may be underprovided through income deficiencies.

9. Tight planning controls in the South East and the uniform business rate are two policies which should encourage expansion in the provinces. By the early 1990s there should be a substantial transformation of the regional situation in the UK, with the eventual solution of many of the traditional regional problems.

5

PRODUCTIVITY IN BRITISH INDUSTRY UNDER MRS THATCHER

Jonathan Haskel and John Kay

Centre for Business Strategy,
London Business School

Introduction

A STUDENT OF BRITAIN'S economic performance who had slept through the arguments of the last decade would be hard pressed to discover what all the fuss has been about. Between 1979 and 1989 GDP has grown at an average rate of 2·3 per cent per annum—slightly better than the 1970s, somewhat worse than the 1960s, and very much in line with the long-term historical performance of the British economy. The growth of manufacturing output has been less than 1 per cent per annum over the same period. Inflation was running a little above OECD averages when Mrs Thatcher was elected and is currently still a little above. Unemployment is rather higher. This is not a bad outcome, but it is not a renaissance or a miracle.

But there is one central observation which the critics of Conservative economic policies find hard to refute. Since the recession of 1982, productivity in British manufacturing industry has grown at an average rate of 5·4 per cent per annum. This is exceptional by British historical standards, impressive by international standards, and a rate of increase which—at the time of writing—appears still to be sustained. This paper has two closely related objectives. It asks what are the causes of that growth. It then examines the extent to which they are

TABLE 1

UK ECONOMY: SELECTED MACRO AGGREGATES

	1979	1980	1981	1982	1983	1984	1985	1986	1987	1988	1989*	Averages			
												1973-79	1979-89	1979-82	1982-89
GDP Growth %	3	-2·8	-1·6	1·7	3·2	3·3	3·7	3·0	4·8	4·5	2·4	2·0	2·3	0·1	3·3
Mfg. Growth %	-0·2	-8·7	-6	0·2	2·9	4	2·8	1·1	5·6	4·5	4·0	0·8	0·9	-3·7	3·1
Mfg. Output/Head Growth %	0·48	-3·9	3·4	6·7	8·5	5·8	2·8	3·0	6·9	4·9	4·9	1·9	3·9	1·7	5·4
Unemployment %	4·0	5·1	8·1	9·5	10·5	10·7	10·9	11·1	10·0	8·0	6·3	3·4	8·6	6·7	9·6
Inflation %	13·5	18·0	11·9	8·6	4·5	5·0	6·0	3·4	4·2	4·9	7·6	14·3	8·0	13·0	5·5

Note: *denotes a forecast; source: *Economic Outlook*, October 1989.

Sources: Economic Trends, Annual Supplement; Department of Employment Gazette.

likely to continue. The answer to the second question is clearly contingent on the answer to the first.

We shall outline a number of causes and argue that the most important contribution has come not from changes in the structure of industry or in the quality of labour or capital employed but from the improved use of existing inputs. We suggest that this is indeed attributable to the supply-side policies the Government has implemented. But if these supply-side measures have obtained increased output from existing inputs, how long can the productivity performance be sustained? A long-run increase in productivity will only result from improvements in the inputs themselves, from education and training to improve labour and from research and development to improve capital. In those areas little change has occurred. This suggests the real possibility that the Thatcher productivity miracle may be running out of steam.

The British Economy since 1979

The last decade has seen considerable vicissitudes in the UK economy (Table 1). Over the whole decade, growth of GDP and manufacturing output are little changed from the 1970s. However, there are two clear sub-periods—from 1979-82 and 1982-89.[1] In the first three Thatcher years, GDP fell by almost 3 per cent, and manufacturing output by over 14 per cent. Since then there has been a marked recovery with sustained growth since 1983. The difference between the two sub-periods is even more distinct if we consider the record of manufacturing output per head, where output is measured with more precision. The average growth rate since 1983 has been a remarkable 5·4 per cent.

The unemployment record is poor, with levels persistently above those of the 1970s, although there has been considerable improvement in recent years. Inflation rose initially, aggravated by a switch from income tax to VAT and by the second oil shock, but fell more or less steadily from 1980 to 1986. Since then, however, inflation has again accelerated.

The overall picture is clear. The British economy suffered a massive recession in 1980-82. Since then there has been a recovery associated with a sustained increase in manufacturing productivity. With an

---

[1] The data for 1989 are from the latest LBS forecast for the UK economy. Recomputing the figures using the 1988 data does not change the picture.

TABLE 2

INTERNATIONAL COMPARISON OF
GDP PER PERSON EMPLOYED
(*per cent per annum*)

	1960-68	1968-73	1973-79	1979-88	1979-82	1982-88
UK	2·7	3·0	1·3	2·2	1·7	2·7
Japan	8·8	7·3	2·9	3·1	3·0	3·0
Germany	4·2	4·1	2·9	1·7	1·1	1·9
France	4·9	4·7	2·7	2·2	2·3	2·2
Italy	6·3	4·9	1·7	2·3	2·2	2·1
USA	2·6	1·0	0·0	1·1	0·5	1·0

Note: For USA, Germany and Japan, pre-1979 figures are for GNP.

Source: OECD, *Historical Statistics*, and *National Institute Economic Review*, August 1989.

indifferent unemployment and inflation record, the jewel in the crown of Britain's economic performance in the 1980s is the growth of productivity.

It is useful to put this performance in some context. Historically, Britain's poor productivity performance over the last century is well known (Feinstein, 1988, Table 2). More recent data are provided in Table 2. As the top row shows, the UK's performance in 1982-88, whilst better than in 1973-79 and 1979-82, was no better than in 1960-73. However, if we compare the UK record across countries, we can see that although during the period 1960-79 Britain was one of the worst-performing of major Western economies, since 1982 the British record has been second only to that of Japan. So whilst a German or Japanese may not be impressed with a growth record of 2·7 per cent, they would be struck by our considerable comparative improvement.[2]

The Causes of Productivity Increase

The observation that productivity has increased over this period may be explained from a number of different sources:

---

[2] We shall concentrate on the record in manufacturing since output measurement is more tentative in the services sector. But it is worth noting that, on the basis of the data we do have, there have been improvements in performance in the non-manufacturing sectors (Bean and Symons, 1989). Privatised industries have led these improvements (Bishop and Kay, 1988).

(i) The movement of labour to above-average sectors, or the 'batting average effect'.

(ii) Growth of capital per head.

(iii) Improved innovation.

(iv) More effective use of inputs.

Beginning with the 'batting average effect', the argument is that if the innings ends before the tail-enders come to the wicket, the average will improve but the score will not. If the 1980s has seen the movement of labour away from below-average industries then the improvement in the aggregate figure may reflect this averaging effect. To examine this question, Haskel and Kay (1989) perform a decomposition of productivity growth using 81 industries for 1981-86. It turns out that there is little contribution from restructuring; indeed in some of the years the movement of labour is to the below-average sectors. This result supports that of Oulton (1987), who examined movement between small and large firms in manufacturing. He found that for 1982 and 1984 large firms had higher productivity levels relative to the average but labour had predominantly moved away from large firms. Thus, if anything it is the opening batsmen who have remained in the pavilion.

Has productivity increased because of an increase in capital per head employed in British industry? This hypothesis is very difficult to support. Investment has been low during the period (Haskel and Kay, 1989), and estimates of total factor productivity therefore show the same trend as movements in labour productivity, even after correcting for hours and mismeasurement of capital due to scrapping (Bean and Symons, 1989, and Muellbauer, 1986).

What of the possibilities of increases in the rate of innovation? Journalism and bar-room discussion abound with suggestions that microchips have dramatic effects on productivity and employment. Table 3 sets out the facts on research and development expenditure from a roughly tri-annual survey of R&D spending in firms conducted by the Business Statistics Office. This represents the most detailed study of R&D in the UK. Expenditure remained almost constant between 1978 and 1983. Since 1983 it has grown by about 10 per cent and this is the period over which productivity has accelerated. Hence the timing of these expenditures follows the pattern of productivity growth. But it is hard to believe that such a modest increase should

TABLE 3

UK RESEARCH AND DEVELOPMENT

	1966	1967	1968	1969	1972	1975	1978	1981	1983	1985
All manufactured products: £m. (1981 prices)	3,332·1	3,354·7	3,347·9	3,364·6	3,104·7	2,917·8	3,409·5	3,511·7	3,322·9	3,656·0
of which % accounted for by:										
electronics	20·0	20·2	20·0	20·7	21·9	21·6	29·6	35·2	38·1	37·1
mechanical engineering	10·3	10·1	9·9	8·9	6·8	8·0	7·4	6·6	6·3	5·5
of which % funded by:										
government	29	29	30	31	33	31	29	30	30	23
overseas	4	4	4	5	6	6	8	9	7	11
Employment in R&D (000's)		219	216	212	183	181	190	195	186	173
of which %:										
scientists and engineers					33	34	36	39	–	47
technicians, lab. assistants					35	34	34	34	–	29
admin., clerical and other					32	32	31	2	–	24

Sources: Industries' Research and Development Expenditure and Employment, London: HMSO, 1981 and 1985.

have had such an immediate impact: more plausibly, the causation runs from performance to R&D spending.

Furthermore, Englander and Mittelstadt (1988) show that our expenditure on R&D as a proportion of GNP has fallen relative to our OECD neighbours, which is inconsistent with our relative improvement.[3]

It would therefore appear that the only explanation left is an increase in the effectiveness with which capital and labour are utilised, and to this we now turn.

The Effectiveness of Capital and Labour

The results of the previous section suggest that it is the more effective use of inputs over the 1980s that are at the heart of the explanation of the improvement in productivity growth. There are various dimensions to this point. The simplest is that workers now work harder, and there is some evidence to support this contention. The percentage utilisation of labour (PUL) index, based on work-study data which seeks to analyse the intensity of physical effort by manual employees, shows a marked rise in the early 1980s (Metcalf, 1988). But changes in the way work and production are organised is almost certainly more significant. There is growing evidence of this (ACAS, 1989, and Metcalf, 1988, for example). In addition, Cross (1988) presents survey evidence which shows that changes have been proceeding at a faster pace than before.

Why might these changes have occurred? There are three main hypotheses.

o The 'shock hypothesis', associated with Metcalf (1988), for example, argues that the huge recession in 1980-81 caused a change in attitudes of workers and managers at the workplace.

o There has been a change in conditions in the labour market; large-scale unemployment and anti-union legislation of the 1980s were responsible for reining back union power and this caused an increase in flexibility and decrease in overmanning among workers.

o There has been a change in conditions in the product market;

---

[3] Haskel and Kay (1989) examine the issue of technical progress further by analysing time-series information on innovations both used and produced by manufacturing. This is based on a survey conducted by the University of Sussex. Following a period of stability in the mid- to late-1970s, there is a sharp decline in both series in the 1980s, suggesting that improved innovation is not a feature of the recent past.

TABLE 4

PRODUCTIVITY GROWTH BY CHARACTERISTICS

	Average growth in output per head, 1982-86 per cent	
Industries in sample	5·4	
Industries in sample about 1980 mean	*above*	*below*
(a) shock	5·8	5·0
(b) labour market characteristics:		
union coverage	4·4	6·6
union density	4·5	7·2
ratio of non-manual to manual	6·2	4·5
(c) product market characteristics:		
concentration ratio (5 firms)	5·9	5·0
proportion of large firms	5·4	5·4
import intensity	6·0	5·0
export intensity	6·2	4·8

increased competition may have forced managements to impose work practice reforms, and unions to accept them.

To investigate these theories, we obtained data for a panel of 81 industries over the 1980s and have taken a number of measures of the 'shock', and of labour and product market conditions in 1980 in each industry. We then calculated average productivity growth, in 1982-86, for industries above and below the average of the particular measure. Our results are set out in Table 4.

It is clear that the productivity gains are greatest in those industries which were seriously affected by the 1979-82 'shock' and which are subject to international competition. The effect of other supply-side variables is more ambiguous. Performance is better in industries with higher concentration, with high proportions of non-manual staff, and with low levels of unionisation. It does not appear that the growth of small firms has been an important factor in the 'productivity miracle'.

Table 5 explores these issues more carefully and emphasises the effect of the interaction between macro-economic shock and product market competition. It suggests that the shock has an effect only if it

TABLE 5

PRODUCTIVITY GROWTH IN INDUSTRIES

Dependent variable: rate of productivity growth

Independent variables	
Capital/labour growth	0·48
	(7·76)
Import intensity	0·26
	(2·69)
Shock x import intensity	−0·27
	(2·66)
Concentration	−0·006
	(0·18)

Notes:

(i) The shock variable is the percentage change in employment from 1979-82. Import intensity is import/(sales + imports − exports).

(ii) Equations include fixed effects (absolute t statistics).

hits industries that are already competitive. Other studies of these hypotheses show the same thrust of results on a variety of different data sets. On the shock effect, Metcalf (1988) finds that industries which experienced the biggest shock have had the largest productivity gains; Bean and Symons (1989) and Layard and Nickell (1989) obtain similar results.

The impact of conditions in the labour market, and trade unions in particular, has been addressed directly in a number of papers. Bean and Symons (1989), using industry data, found that unionised industries showed the strongest accelerations in total factor productivity (TFP) growth between 1973-79 and 1980-86. Similar results are reported by Denny and Muellbauer (1988); they found productivity growth positively related to unionisation. Using data on firms, Nickell, Wadhwani and Wall (1989) found that union firms had higher growth in 1980-84, and Machin and Wadhwani (1989) (using data from the Workplace Industrial Relations Survey) concluded that '. . . substantial changes in work organisation or work practices . . .' had been introduced to a greater extent in unionised workplaces.

The impact of reforms in product markets has received comparatively little attention. As Table 5 shows, our results suggest that industries facing increased competition from imports over the 1980s

TABLE 6

TOTAL FACTOR PRODUCTIVITY IN UK PUBLIC SECTOR

| | Annual rate of increase (per cent) | | |
	1979-88	1979-83	1983-88
BAA	1·6	0·0	2·8
British Coal*	2·9	0·6	4·6
British Gas	3·3	−0·2	6·2
British Rail	1·3	−0·4	2·7
British Steel	12·9	8·4	12·4
British Telecom	2·4	2·0	2·5
Electricity supply	1·4	−1·6	4·0
Post Office	3·7	3·6	3·3
Average	*3·7*	*1·6*	*4·8*

*Adjusted for effects of 1984-85 coal miners' strike.

Source: Bishop & Kay (1989).

had better performance. Nickell, Wadhwani and Wall (1989) found that large firms had higher productivity growth in the 1980s, and Machin and Wadhwani (1989) found that they were more likely to introduce change at the workplace. Bean and Symons found that growth was higher in industries dominated by large firms.[4] Both results are consistent with the idea that the potential for gains was greatest in firms with market power.

One of the most profound supply-side reforms is the privatisation programme. In Table 6 we examine evidence on the performance of these firms. There is a marked break in trend around 1982-83 when the programme began, and the growth of productivity over the later period has been strong across the sector. It is notable, however, that performance has improved whether the industry was privatised or not—for example, British Telecom and British Steel respectively. This evidence suggests that the contribution of privatisation as such is rather limited. However, privatisation and deregulation have contributed to the general climate of a more commercial approach to management, which has improved performance.

We believe the evidence described above is broadly favourable to

---

[4] They argue that firm size is a proxy for multi-unionism.

the 'supply-side' argument. Productivity has improved, particularly in industries which were subject to a macro-economic shock, unionised and vulnerable to competition. The improvements are clearest where the supply-side view indicates there was most scope—in concentrated industries and in previously protected areas of the public sector. This overall assessment cannot be conclusive because of the difficulties of measurement of many of these factors, but the general direction of change seems clear.

The Lessons

The conclusions of this analysis present a mixture of good news and bad news, either for those who are convinced supporters of 'supply-side economics' or for those who are anxious to ensure that the improvements in Britain's economic performance in the 1980s are sustained into the next decade.

The good news is that there is evidence that supply-side policies work. As we have seen, improvements have occurred in industries where union power was high at the start of the decade, and whose product markets were protected and uncompetitive. The archetypes of industries where dramatic productivity improvements have occurred— steel, coal, newspapers—are indeed archetypes. The policies have worked, however, mostly by squeezing out inefficiency. The source of concern is that all these are *exhaustible* sources of productivity gain and, moreover, ones in which the more gains have been made the harder it becomes to gain more. A long-term break in trend in productivity growth requires not so much a change in the efficiency with which existing inputs are used as a change in the quality of inputs themselves.

The evidence on these fundamental inputs makes for a less promising outlook. On the capital/technical progress side, we have already reviewed the evidence on R&D and innovations (Table 4). Despite some recent growth, the lost ground in the early 1980s and our poor relative performance do not bode well for prospects of productivity growth. As for labour, we see education and training as key indicators. Some comparative data are set out in Table 7, which shows the UK lagging behind on every measure of human capital acquisition. We have a lower proportion of 16-24 year-olds in education and even those in education obtain lower qualifications. As for the quality of the workforce, our training expenditures per head are low by international standards. Finally, the proportion of managers

TABLE 7

INTERNATIONAL COMPARISONS OF
HUMAN CAPITAL ACQUISITION

		UK	W. Germany	France	Japan	USA
(a)	Population aged 16-24 years and participating in education (%)	36	45	–	54	73
(b)	Highest qualification of school leavers (%)					
	University entrance level	15	30	35	–	–
	Intermediate and low level	75	60	55	–	–
	No qualifications	10	10	10	–	–
(c)	Number qualifying in engineering and technology, per head of population, 1985					
	Bachelor degree	14	21	15	35	–
	Technician	29	44	35	36	–
	Craftsman	35	120	92	58	–
(d)	Levels of training expenditure by employers, 1986 (£ per head)	800	850	–	–	1,400
(e)	Management education					
	Top managers with degrees (%)	24	62	65	85	85

Notes and sources of headings:
(a) UK and USA data for 1981, Germany 1980, Japan 1982. Japan's official school-leaving age is 16, data is 15-23 age-group. *Source*: NEDO (1984).
(b) First row is 2 A-levels and above, second is 1 A-level to below O-level. *Source*: CBI (1989).
(c) *Source*: CBI (1989).   (d) *Source*: CBI (1988).
(e) Data for Britain is 1975, Germany 1982, Japan 1975 and USA 1986. *Source*: Handy *et al.* (1988), who also report more recent data for Britain. In the 1985 Labour Force Survey, 12% of those calling themselves managers had degrees. A 1987 CBI survey of corporate managers reported 40%.

with a degree is at the bottom of the list. In general, therefore, there seems little in the record of the 1980s to suggest that an improvement in input quality has occurred, or is in prospect.

REFERENCES

ACAS (1988): *Labour Flexibility in Britain: The 1987 ACAS Survey*, Occasional Paper 41.

Bean, C. and J. Symons (1989): 'Ten Years of Mrs T', *CEPR Discussion Paper* No. 316, April, and *NBER Macroeconomics Annual*, forthcoming.

Bishop, M. and J. Kay (1988): *Does Privatization Work? Lessons from the UK*, Centre for Business Strategy, London Business School.

Confederation of British Industry (1989): *Towards a Skills Revolution*, London: CBI.

Confederation of British Industry (1988): *Skills for Success*, London: CBI.

Cross, M. (1988): 'Changes in Working Practices in UK Manufacturing 1987-88', *Industrial Relations Review and Report*, 5 May.

Denny, K. and J. Muellbauer (1988): 'Economic and Industrial Relations: Explanations for Productivity Change', Oxford: Nuffield College (mimeo).

Englander, A. S. and A. Mittelstadt (1988): 'Total Factor Productivity: Macroeconomic and Structural Aspects of the Slowdown', *Economic Studies*, No. 10, OECD, Spring.

Feinstein, C. (1988): 'Economic Growth Since 1870: Britain's Performance in International Perspective', *Oxford Review of Economic Policy*, Vol. 4, No. 1.

Handy, C. *et al.* (1988): *Making Managers*, London: Pitman.

Haskel, J. and J. Kay (1989): 'Mrs Thatcher's Economic Experiment: Lessons from the UK', paper presented at the Australian Economic Policy Conference, Canberra.

Layard, R. and S. Nickell (1989): 'The Thatcher Miracle?', *American Economic Review*, Papers and Proceedings, May.

Machin, S. and S. Wadhawani (1989): 'The Effect of Unions on Organisational Change, Investment and Employment: Evidence from WIRS', Centre for Labour Economics Discussion Paper No. 355, London School of Economics.

Metcalf, D. (1988): 'Water Notes Dry Up', Centre for Labour Economics Discussion Paper No. 314, London School of Economics.

Muellbauer, J. (1986): 'The Assessment: Productivity and Competitiveness in UK Manufacturing', *Oxford Review of Economic Policy*, Vol. 2, No. 3.

National Economic Development Office (1984): *Competence and Competition*, London: NEDO.

Nickell, S., S. Wadhwani and M. Wall (1989): 'Unions and Productivity Growth in Britain in the 70s and 80s: Evidence from Company Accounts Data', Centre for Labour Economics Discussion Paper No. 353, London School of Economics.

Oulton, N. (1987): 'Plant Closures and the Productivity Miracle in Manufacturing', *National Institute Review*, No. 121.

6

WHAT WENT WRONG? HOW TO PUT IT RIGHT? MONETARY CONTROL, PAST, PRESENT AND FUTURE

Gordon Pepper

City University Business School

What Went Wrong?

THE UNDERLYING RATE of inflation—that is, excluding mortgage interest—has risen from 3·5 per cent in the year to February 1988 to over 6 per cent in the year to November 1989. There has also been a huge deterioration in the current account of the balance of payments, some of which represents inflation in the pipeline that has yet to come out into the open.

The prime role of monetary policy is to control inflation. There has clearly been a definite failure. There is no need to go into the detail of the behaviour of the different monetary aggregates. The fact is that monetary policy failed in its primary purpose.

The failure was particularly acute as the most important reason for the excessive monetary growth which the authorities allowed to occur was buoyancy of credit. If the reason had been a huge budget deficit, it could have been argued that fiscal policy was partly to blame. As it was borrowing by the private sector, the fault lies wholly with monetary policy.

The failure to stop inflation from rising is very disappointing given the Prime Minister's determination to prevent it. The failure is not one of political resolve but of *technique* of monetary control.

A distinction should be drawn between the recent rise in inflation and the Government's failure in 1985 to take advantage of falling oil prices virtually to eliminate inflation. In 1985 a deliberate political decision may well have been taken that it was worth postponing a further fall in inflation for a year or so for the sake of economic growth. In the recent case, in contrast, the political resolve was, surely, not to run the risk of a significant rise in inflation.

How to Put it Right?

There are two options. The first would be to change the domestic technique of monetary control to one which would be robust and reliable. The second would be to hand over responsibility for monetary policy to an external body that would be capable, i.e. to the Bundesbank.

External Choice

The second option would mean the UK joining the Exchange Rate Mechanism (ERM) of the European Monetary System (EMS) and, further, following a policy of not 'sterilising' any foreign exchange outflow. Intervention in the foreign exchange market is said to be sterilised if its impact on the money supply is offset by official operations in the gilt-edged market. A policy of refraining from sterilisation would mean that intervention in the foreign exchange market to stop sterling from falling below its band would reduce the money supply—that is, monetary policy would automatically be tightened. The discipline would be similar to that of the pre-1914 Gold Standard. (A decision to join the ERM and continue with the present policy of sterilisation would be neither one thing nor the other. It would allow the UK to escape discipline for a time. It would be the worst choice. Sir Alan Walters's description of it as 'half-baked' is a good one.)

Domestic Choice

Continuing with the European theme, competition between currencies has been put forward as an alternative to an early move to a common currency as proposed by the Delors Report. *Sterling would have no chance of competing successfully against the deutschemark—the Bank of England would not have any hope in a contest with the Bundesbank—if the present system of monetary control remains.* The Bank's only chance would be to go one better than the Bundesbank and adopt the control mechanism of the Swiss National Bank.

The Present System

Under the present system in the UK the authorities follow a demand-side rather than a supply-side approach. They consider that the best way of controlling the amount of money in existence is to influence people's demand for it. This is done by varying interest rates. Accordingly, the Bank of England alters interest rates to the level at which the authorities estimate that people's demand for money will fall into line with the target for the money stock. If the authorities get their estimates wrong or if there is an unexpected alteration in one of the other factors influencing the demand for money, for example in the rate of inflation or in the rate of growth of the economy, the money stock will depart from its target path. This is what has been happening.

The Proposed System

Under the Swiss system the central bank adopts a supply-side approach, that is, it influences the supply of money directly. This is done by controlling the quantity of reserves available to the banking system. If the quantity of reserves is strictly limited, the total of banks' balance sheets will ultimately be controlled and, hence, the supply of money.

Under the UK's present system the supply of bank reserves is, in effect, without limit. To understand this, it is necessary to appreciate a sequence. The starting point is that a bank can easily persuade one of its customers to issue a commercial bill rather than take a loan; all that is needed is a very slightly lower interest rate. After the commercial bill has been issued, the next step is for it to be 'accepted' (i.e. guaranteed) by the bank and by a discount house. It then becomes a 'primary liquid asset'. The important point is that the total quantity of these primary liquid assets is under the control of banks and not the Bank of England.

The second important feature is that the Bank stands ready in all circumstances either to encash these primary liquid assets or to accept them as collateral for last-resort lending. This is the guarantee of liquidity behind the inter-bank market. It is the reason why bankers can be completely confident that they will always be able to obtain whatever funds they need in that market. The banks' only requirement for balances with the Bank of England is virtually confined to covering errors in the daily forecasts of Exchequer transactions.

To summarise, the Bank's willingness to encash primary liquid assets means that the inter-bank market is so liquid that banks have absolutely minimal need for reserves. Further, supply of primary liquid assets is unlimited.

The crucial operational change under the proposed system would be that the Bank would decide on the size of its transactions in the bill and money markets rather than passively allow banks and discount houses to deal in whatever amount they wanted. Primary liquid assets would, accordingly, become less liquid and banks would have a much greater need to hold balances with the Bank.

There would be two possible approaches to controlling the quantity of reserves available to banks. The first would be to restrict the definition of reserve assets to ones which could not be 'manufactured' by the banking sector. There would have to be a mandatory ratio for these (to stop banks from relying on 'manufactured assets'). The Bank would control total reserves by buying or selling qualifying assets in the market.

The second, and much simpler, approach would be to concentrate on bankers' balances at the Bank. Because the central bank is the only ultimate source of liquidity, there would be no need for an artificial definition of reserves. Even a mandatory ratio would be unnecessary. If the Bank were to control the growth of its own liabilities, it would control the liquidity of the financial system as a whole. The Bank could control the growth of its own balance sheet by buying or selling assets. This is how it would determine the size of its transactions in the bill and money markets.

Discipline

Financial discipline is fundamental to the control of inflation. Control of the money supply implies a tight constraint on the rate of growth of the balance sheet of the banking sector as a whole. Even more basic is control of the rate of growth of the central bank's own balance sheet. Discipline should start at the top. *The Bank of England's unwillingness to control the growth of its own balance sheet is the fundamental reason why monetary policy in the UK has so far had no firm foundation.*

The Debate

The Conservatives came to power in May 1979. The argument that monetary policy should be based on a firm foundation raged throughout their first year of office. The Bank's first public response was an article, 'Monetary base control', by Foot, Goodhart and Hotson, in its June 1979 *Quarterly Bulletin*. The Green Paper, *Monetary Control* (Cmnd. 7858), followed in March 1980. Another notable event was a seminar at Church House, Westminster, chaired jointly by Mr Peter Middleton (since knighted and promoted to Permanent Secretary of the Treasury) and Mr John Fforde (executive director of the Bank of England in charge of domestic monetary policy and now retired). The decision was eventually taken at Prime Ministerial level. It was that the old demand-side approach should continue.

There was an attempt to re-open the debate shortly after the Conservatives won a second term of office in June 1983. The important personnel had changed. Mr Nigel Lawson had succeeded Sir Geoffrey Howe as Chancellor of the Exchequer, Mr Robin Leigh-Pemberton was the new Governor and, importantly, Mr Eddie George had taken over responsibility for domestic monetary policy from Mr Fforde. Disappointingly, the advocates of a firm foundation lost again. They did so because they could not answer an important practical point. The Bank would inevitably have to be in charge of implementing the change to the new system and the Bank remained implacably hostile.

Foreign Exchange Intervention

A subsequent important event was the start of massive intervention in the foreign exchange market in February 1987. This was supposedly under the Louvre Accord, to support the dollar, but the fact is that the amount of the intervention which the UK authorities chose to make was precisely that needed to peg sterling's exchange rate against the deutschemark just below 3·0. There was, of course, a Common Market reason for wanting to peg sterling to the deutschemark but another possibility was that Mr Lawson had lost confidence in the domestic mechanism for monetary control and wished to replace it by an external discipline.

The Right Choice

Anyone whose vision of Europe is not the federal one of Delors, who believes that 'more haste, less speed' may well apply to a common currency (i.e. that imposing a common currency before economies have grown more closely together could easily provoke a political backlash), and who accepts the technical argument that the present arrangements under the ERM are 'half-baked', should agree that Mr Lawson chose the wrong option. He should have chosen the domestic solution and insisted on the Bank of England accepting the discipline of controlling its own balance sheet. This would have based monetary policy on a firm foundation.

7

EUROPEAN MONETARY INTEGRATION IN THE 1990s
The Importance of the Legal-Tender
Status of European Currencies
Tim Congdon
Gerrard & National

Vagueness about Meaning of European Monetary Integration

THE DEBATE about European monetary integration has been complicated and at times acrimonious, but in many ways it has not been properly joined. Political leaders throughout Europe often use summits, inter-governmental conferences and the like to put together phrases about the benefits of greater monetary integration. These phrases tend to be visionary, vague and rhetorical. The sceptics' reaction is to ask 'What do you mean?'. This seems to cause resentment, partly perhaps from a feeling that nothing can be done if there is bickering about detail from the start. (The sceptics in this context include the British Government and the Bundesbank.)

Legal-Tender Status of New European Currency Is Critical

Despite the tensions about the implications of the debate, there is widespread agreement that the debate itself will be crucial in defining the UK's position in Europe throughout the 1990s. The purpose of this paper is to improve the discussion by suggesting how the general question 'What do you mean?' can be transformed into a specific choice between institutional alternatives. Enthusiasts for greater monetary integration need to be confronted with a question on the lines 'Are you for or against X?', where X is a particular institutional arrangement. The argument here is that the key characteristic differentiating various possible arrangements is the legal-tender status of the proposed European currency. Curiously, this characteristic has not yet played much of a role in the debate. Its importance will be made clear if some basic ideas in the analysis of different monetary systems are outlined. Once this has been done, it will become possible to put forward a number of specific institutional options and to consider their implications.

The notion of a 'legal tender' tends to be taken for granted in sophisticated modern economies, but in fact it has not always been found in the past. In primitive economies, where government is weak and the rule of law is not well-established, people may refuse to accept payment in the 'money' declared to be legal tender by the state. The problem is least severe if the money is a commodity with intrinsic value. Clearly, if a monetary unit is measured as having a particular weight of gold, silver or whatever, it does not need legal-tender status for it to be of known value and therefore useful in transactions.

Legal-Tender Status Essential for Paper Money

But, as economies evolved from commodity money to paper money, legal-tender status became essential. In the 18th century the Bank of England issued notes, but these were not legal tender and only circulated widely because of the belief—justified for most of the time— that they could be converted into gold. In the early 19th century Bank of England notes were declared to be legal tender, but continued to be convertible into gold, which gave an ultimate guarantee of value. Finally, in 1931 Britain left the gold standard. The Bank's notes nevertheless remained legal tender. They have been fully acceptable in payment ever since and are rightly described as the 'monetary base' on which all credit expansion and deposit creation depend.

The key point about legal tender is that refusal to accept it in payment breaks the law. People accept bits of paper (which have almost no value in their own right) in payment for goods and services (which have obvious value) only because a powerful and effective state is able to enforce the legal-tender laws. Thus, since 1931 a one-pound note has been worth one pound not because of its form as a commodity (since the paper is practically worthless), but because the British Government is prepared to punish anyone who denies that it is worth one pound. The Government's role is decisive. If the

Government had not passed the legal-tender laws, people would not regard pound notes as an acceptable medium of exchange and they would not be 'money' in the usually understood sense.

New European Currency Will Not Be Acceptable Medium of Exchange Unless Backed by Legal-Tender Status

How is this point relevant to European monetary integration? The answer is that a European currency will not be an acceptable medium of exchange unless it is also legal tender. Further, the Governments of the EC will make no progress on monetary integration unless they decide—sooner or later—to make the chosen European 'money' legal tender in their countries. If it is ever taken, the decision to confer legal-tender status on the favoured 'money' will be the watershed in European monetary integration.

Delors Silent on Legal-Tender Implications of Its Proposals

The emphasis placed here on the legal-tender aspect of money is not found in the Delors Report. Its Stage One envisaged all community currencies joining the exchange rate mechanism of the EMS, the removal of exchange controls and a doubling of the resources of EC regional aid funds. Stage Two is seen as transitional, involving the establishment of the European System of Central Banks (ESCB). Only at the end of the Third Stage would a single European currency be instituted. Essential preliminaries to the Third Stage are listed as the irrevocable locking of exchange rates, the transfer of responsibility for monetary policy to the ESCB and the imposition of constraints on national budgets. The Report recognises that, since Stage Three would require amendment to the Treaty of Rome, it would oblige member-states to change their constitutional laws and pass new monetary legislation. But it does not highlight revision to the legal-tender laws as the critical change, as it ought to have done.

UK Treasury Aware of Importance of Legal Tender and Supports 'Currency Competition'

By contrast, the UK Treasury has shown an acute awareness that the question of legal tender is central to the debate. Last year it put up a proposal for 'currency competition' as an alternative to Delors at the Antibes meeting of EC finance ministers. The essence of the proposal was that all EC currencies should be legal tender in all EC states, a revolutionary change from the present position where each currency is

91

legal tender only in its country of issue. The idea was to initiate a process of 'may the best currency win', in the conviction that the general publics of the various European countries would select 'the' European currency by using it more frequently in transactions than the alternatives. The finance ministers from other European countries were puzzled and unimpressed by the proposal, which made no headway at all. As we shall argue below, they were right to be suspicious. However, it did have the virtue—unlike the Delors Report—of focussing on the legal-tender characteristic of money.

(It should be noted that the Treasury's concept of currency competition—that is, of trans-continental legal tender—is not the same as the abolition of exchange controls—that is, Stage One of Delors—as some newspapers have suggested. If exchange controls are removed in a particular European country, it is no longer illegal to use other EC currencies in transactions, as a unit of account and so on. But it would continue to be legal to refuse payment in such currencies. With trans-continental legal tender, it would be illegal to refuse payment in them. The difference is basic.)

A European Central Bank Would Issue Note Liabilities, Which Might or Might not Be Legal Tender; Four Alternative Proposals

In modern circumstances legal tender is in the form of either notes, when it is the liability of a central bank, or coin, when it is the liability of a mint. Since the note issue is much the larger of the two in all European countries, the discussion can proceed as if notes alone were relevant. If there is to be a European currency, it will have to be a liability of a European central bank which issues legal-tender notes. A range of options, differentiated by the extent to which this note issue and the various national note issues are accorded legal-tender status, can then be considered and related to the Delors agenda.

Four alternatives will be discussed:

1. Notes issued by the European central bank (ECB) are not legal tender in any EC member-state.

2. Notes issued by the European central bank are legal tender, but national central banks continue and their notes remain legal tender in their own countries. These national notes are legal tender only in the country of issue, not elsewhere in Europe.

3. Notes issued by the European central bank are legal tender, but

national central banks continue and their notes become legal tender in all European countries.

4. The European central bank becomes a currency monopolist, with only its notes remaining as legal tender. National notes are deprived of legal-tender status in their original country of issue.

First Proposal: ECB's notes not legal tender

The first proposal is the least interesting. As already explained, if the European currency does not acquire legal-tender status, it will not be used as a medium of exchange. It will not become a genuine 'money'. The ECB will be merely another banking institution, except that its accounts and operations will be denominated in the European currency rather than a national currency. It will be rather like the present European Investment Bank (EIB), whose accounts are expressed in terms of European Currency Units (ECUs) but which otherwise has a closer resemblance to a commercial bank than a central bank. In fact, without legal-tender status for its liabilities, the European central bank would not advance beyond its present role and would be merely a glorified EIB.

Support for this claim comes from the EC's failure to develop the ECU as a meaningful 'money' since it was introduced over 10 years ago. True enough, the ECU is widely, and increasingly, used as a unit of account in international capital markets. But nowhere in Europe is it a medium of exchange. The ECU's subordinate position in the European financial scene persists despite repeated official attempts in some countries to encourage its greater use in private transactions. The Italians have been particularly active in this area and have long allowed citizens to hold bank accounts in ECUs, but not in other foreign currencies. In contrast, the Bundesbank has always disparaged the ECU. Indeed, for many years West Germany did not allow its citizens to open bank accounts in ECU or make bank transfers in it.

Second Proposal: ECB's notes legal tender alongside
only one national currency in each EC member-state

The second proposal is that the note liabilities of the ECB are made legal tender throughout the EC, alongside the existing national currencies which remain legal tender. In these circumstances the European currency would probably be used in some transactions, particularly in cross-border trade. It would therefore become, at least to some degree, a medium of exchange. Its role in international capital markets would also expand, increasing the potential for ECU clearing business. There are, however, two serious objections to this proposal.

The first is that there is a tendency for transactors in any market to standardise on one unit of account. This tendency was first described by the Austrian economist, Carl Menger, in a famous article, written in the 1890s, on the origins of money. The common sense behind it is obvious. Comparisons of value are complicated if prices are expressed in terms of two monies rather than one. The price mechanism is supposed to bring supply and demand into balance, but if every object has two prices the costs of using the price mechanism are increased. It follows that, when people are already happy with prices expressed in terms of their national currencies, they will be reluctant to set prices in terms of the European currency. The spread of the European currency as a medium of exchange will be impeded.

Secondly, there will be a new task of managing the European currency. Many advocates of a European currency seem to believe that it will easily supplant national currencies, particularly if national central banks continue to pursue inflationary policies. But that depends on what the new European currency is and how it is controlled. If the new currency is a legal-tender ECU, its inflationary performance will be no better than that of the average of the national EC currencies. In the low-inflation countries of the EC the ECU will have no attractions compared with the national currencies; even in the high-inflation countries its merits as a store of value will depend on how far the depreciation of national currencies is outweighed by the interest differential between deposits in ECUs and such currencies. There is nothing inevitable about Europe's citizens wanting to hold vast quantities of ECUs, even if it is legal tender. If the European currency is not to be the ECU but some entirely new instrument, the discussion becomes even more hypothetical. It must be emphasised that the people of Europe will be suspicious of a currency which has no track record.

In practice, there would be a finite demand to hold the European currency, whatever form it took. As with any money, if the supply came to exceed the demand, there would tend to be a loss of value which would be symptomised in a depreciation of the European currency on the foreign exchanges. This would, of course, be catastrophic for its continued viability as a medium of exchange in competition with national currencies. The ECB would therefore have to be prepared to intervene on the foreign exchanges to keep the European currency stable against the various national currencies.

Over-supply of ECB's Note Liabilities Would Lead to Depreciation

This point is immensely important. It explains why Stage Three of the Delors Report envisages irrevocable locking of EC exchange rates and pooling of reserves. It also explains why these proposals are potentially so contentious. Suppose that the ECB expands its balance sheet aggressively in the first few years after its liabilities are granted legal-tender status. Its assets might consist principally of so-called 'structural loans' to poor regions of the EC, extra finance for various EC development funds, the Common Agricultural Policy and the like. Sooner or later the European currency threatens to collapse because it has been over-supplied, with people selling it in order to hold not only more dollars and yen, but also more deutschemarks, pounds, francs and so on.

How would the European central bank react? If it were unable to contract its loans and balance-sheet size, it would have to sell the reserves that the various European countries had left with it. In other words, the reserves would be spent to support a number of European causes with which some governments, including the British Government, have little sympathy. There would be a genuine, and possibly large, transfer of resources between countries, depending on whether they borrowed more from the ECB than they lent to it. (Of course, the point would be most serious if the pooling of reserves involved permanent loss of ownership and/or control of reserves by individual countries, rather than simply lending them to the ECB.)

National Central Banks Might Have to Lend to ECB, with Inflationary Consequences

What would happen if the European Central Bank ran out of deutschemarks, pounds, francs and so on, as it sold these currencies in order to sustain the value of its note liabilities? The answer is that it would go to the various national central banks and ask them for further supplies of their respective currencies. The national central banks could meet these requests by expanding their balance sheets, with potentially inflationary consequences. More generally, unless co-operation between the ECB and the national central banks were

95

remarkably smooth, there would be constant bickering between the various parties concerned about how much the bank could borrow and lend, whom it could lend to and so on. Heavy emphasis needs to be placed on the point that, in a democratic context, such squabbling would be on public view and would undermine the credibility of the European currency. *The demand to hold the currency would be correspondingly limited.*

It should be clear from our discussion that the apparently technical issue of how to operate the European Central Bank is really a political question about which country gets what. This difficulty recurs with the next two proposals and is, in fact, inescapable with any pan-European monetary arrangement.

Third Proposal: ECB's notes legal tender and national currencies become legal tender across Europe

The third proposal is more ambitious and resembles the Treasury's Antibes scheme. It is that legal-tender status be accorded within each EC member-state not only to the note liabilities of the European Central Bank and its own national central bank, but to the note liabilities of all other EC national central banks. In other words, the deutschemark, French franc, lira and so on become legal tender in the UK in addition to the European currency and the pound sterling. The thinking here is that, in a Darwinian competitive contest between currencies, the fittest currency will survive. The proposal has an attractively democratic flavour. Instead of Brussels taking all the decisions, the people of Europe will choose the best currency.

Unhappily, this proposal suffers even more from the two objections raised to the previous suggestion. The argument that transactors standardise on one unit of account is awkward enough if only two currencies, the national and the European, are in competition. But there would be even more trouble if half-a-dozen or more currencies were involved. Indeed, competition between such a large number of currencies would be extraordinarily inconvenient and transactors in each country would surely very quickly narrow down the choice to one or two currencies. (This is not to deny that they might hold deposits denominated in several foreign currencies. But—in EC countries without exchange controls—they can do this at present. To repeat, a currency is not a proper 'money' if it is used only as a store of value. It must also act as a medium of exchange.)

Central Banks Could Export Inflation to Other Countries, Where Their Currencies Are Also Legal Tender

The problem over the relative size of the various central bank balance sheets would also be more serious. With all the currencies jostling against each other, the demand for a particular currency could fluctuate sharply. Unless the central banks were prepared to lend to each other on a massive scale, the fixed exchange rates between their currencies could probably not be maintained. Indeed, there is one argument which seems to be a crushing refutation of this proposal. If the lira is legal tender in West Germany, the Banca d'Italia has an incentive to issue enormous amounts of lira and hope that they will be spent in West Germany. If they are spent in West Germany, they will increase the demand for German goods and services, not Italian, and the inflationary effects will not be confined to Italy. More generally, in a continent whose countries have several legal tenders, the concept of a 'national inflation rate' breaks down.

Concept of 'National Inflation Rate' Breaks Down

But the breakdown of the concept of a 'national inflation rate' is fatal to the idea of currency competition. The purpose of currency competition is to see which central bank is best at keeping inflation down. If comparisons of national inflation rates are no longer possible, currency competition is not viable.

Our analysis of the last two proposals shows how complicated it is to imagine a situation where several currencies are legal tender within the same political unit. The difficulties suggest that there are two valid options, the present one where each currency is legal tender in its nation of issue but nowhere else, and a radical alternative where all the national currencies have disappeared, only one European currency remains and this currency is legal tender across Europe. In both cases there is only one legal tender and, presumably, only one 'money', which agrees with Menger's theory that transactors standardise on one unit. The final proposal is therefore that the European Central Bank becomes Europe's currency monopolist and that its note liabilities alone are legal tender. This could be regarded as the ultimate objective of the Delors Report.

Fourth Proposal: ECB's notes as only legal tender in Europe and ECB becomes Europe's currency monopolist

The discussion of the two versions of currency competition has served a useful purpose by warning that the transition from the present situation to the ultimate Delors goal will be difficult to plan and even, in some respects, difficult to conceptualise. Our argument has been, first, that a currency cannot become a meaningful 'money' unless it has been given the status of legal tender and, second, that competition between several legal tenders in one political unit is liable to be chaotic. It follows that any transition process which envisages a number of co-existing legal tenders—during, say, Delors Stage Two or the early part of Delors Stage Three—should be regarded with considerable scepticism. Indeed, the problem of specifying the transition is so serious that the only way forward appears to be a leap from the present situation to the final situation with the ECB as Europe's monopoly central bank. In this leap the existing national currencies would suffer a sudden death. Is this desirable? Is there any way it could be made to work?

It should be said straightaway that there can be no doubts about the feasibility of a single European currency if there is already a single European government in being. If the leaders of the 12 EC member-states were to agree that at some future date they would surrender sovereignty, and in particular the power to tax, to one European government, an agreement on the unification of monetary systems ought to emerge quickly *after* that one European government had been created. But that is not the issue. Instead the Delors thinking is that a single European currency is to develop *before* a single European government is established. Two kinds of problem must be highlighted, the first connected with the sudden death of existing national currencies and the second with the need to decide which countries lend to the European central bank and which borrow from it.

Practical Difficulties with Sudden Death of National Currencies

The sudden death of existing national currencies would lead to serious inconvenience and confusion, and this inconvenience and confusion would be distributed so arbitrarily between people, companies and nations that the whole idea has to be regarded as impracticable. In the extreme case all the existing currencies lose their legal-tender status overnight. Institutional upheaval on a massive scale would then become necessary. Millions of contracts—insurance policies, bank loans, the terms of bond issues, wills, agreements between customers and suppliers—would have to be revised in short order. These revisions would not be matters merely of form (as with decimalisation), since virtually all contracts have some interest rate content and the adoption of a new currency would mean a change in the effective interest rate. There would be the awkward question of what should be done with public debts, since these differ substantially (as a share of GDP) between European countries. The nature of the relationship between the new European central bank and the banking systems of the individual EC countries (e.g., in terms of reserve ratios, liquidity ratios, access to lender-of-last-resort facilities) would have to be resolved.

Finally, but certainly not least, no one could predict in advance just how large the ECB's balance sheet should be. There would be a danger of rapid inflation if it were too large and deflation if it were too small. In short, the sudden replacement of existing national currencies by one European currency is not practical politics.

Which Governments Are Entitled to Borrow from the ECB?

The question of which countries deposit with the European central bank and which borrow from it, and of the terms and conditions on the various deposits and loans, is also highly problematic. It is related to the question already discussed under the heading of the second proposal, of how the new bank should conduct its business. At present the governments of Italy, Spain and Greece borrow heavily from their central banks and banking systems. With the disappearance of their national central banks, they would presumably seek similar levels of financing from the European central bank. But why should these governments be entitled to borrow more from the European central bank than the governments of the UK and West Germany?

Summary of the Argument: Delors Report Unworkable

The argument can now be summed up. No proposed European currency will be a genuine 'money' unless its acceptability as a medium of exchange is backed up by legal-tender status. We can think of various possibilities. If the liabilities of the new European central bank are not legal tender, it would be nothing more than a glorified European Investment Bank. If they are legal tender and compete with either one currency in each nation (the second proposal) or all national currencies across Europe (the third proposal), the situation would become unstable for a variety of reasons, not least people's preference for a single unit of account. These instabilities warn that a process of gradual transition to a single European currency will be difficult, perhaps unacceptably so. *But the final option, with the sudden death of existing national currencies in order to bring in the new European currency overnight, would be so traumatic as to be politically impossible.*

In short, our attempts to specify how the Delors programme might work in practice fail. Legal-tender status is essential to the acceptance of paper money as money. But, as soon as we ask how legal-tender status is to be introduced in a European context while there are still several independent governments, we encounter insuperable difficulties. The European leaders who support the Delors Report may mean what they say; the trouble is that they do not seem to know what they mean. The right way to demonstrate the vagueness of their thinking is to ask them, 'When do you want the single European currency to become legal tender?', and 'Do you want it to be the only legal tender in Europe or a legal tender in competition with existing national currencies?'. These are the serious questions that need to be answered at the inter-governmental conference on European monetary integration which is due to be held in December 1990.

West Germany Will Reject the Delors Report

In fact, it is already known that they will not be answered. Despite Chancellor Kohl's enthusiasm for the Delors Report for most of last year, the reality is that the Germans are suspicious of European monetary union. According to the *New Europe* newsletter of 21 December 1989, German representatives at the Strasbourg summit were 'dragging their feet' because they were 'worried that the implications of a European banking system have not been sufficiently thought through'. The Bundesbank's probable hostility in future to conferring legal-tender status on a European money is revealed by its active discouragement in the past of the private use of the ECU.

1990s Will Not See European Monetary Union

Mrs Thatcher has taken no risks in rejecting Stages Two and Three of the Delors Report. She has been criticised for keeping the UK out of the European Monetary System and 'missing the boat' to European monetary union. But the EMS and EMU need to be sharply distinguished. Despite continuing currency realignments, the EMS is undoubtedly afloat. But the boat of EMU has never, in a meaningful sense, been launched. Unless and until the proposed European currency is to be accorded legal-tender status and made into a genuine money, all the visionary rhetoric about EMU is just so much waffle. The 1990s will not be a decade of European monetary integration. At the beginning of the 21st century there will still be deutschemarks, pounds, francs, lira, pesetas and so on. Deep down, every European knows this.

8

THE LABOUR MARKET: FALSE START, STRONG FOLLOW-THROUGH AND NOW FOR THE FINISH

Patrick Minford

University of Liverpool

The Thatcher Decade in the Economy and the Labour Market— Was It a Miracle?

BECAUSE OF current monetary difficulties, left-inclined commentators are having a field-day saying nothing has really changed since 1979. The argument goes that if Rip van Winkle had gone to sleep in 1979 and woken up today, he would not blink. Inflation at 7-8 per cent, unemployment at 1·7 million, the balance of payments in deficit to the tune of 3 per cent of GDP: the British disease is as rampant as ever, surely?

Clearly these symptoms—including at least part of the current rise in wage settlements—do owe something to our earlier monetary excess in 1987-88. And certainly monetary excess was a part of the British disease.

But that monetary excess has now been savagely corrected. Furthermore, whereas in 1979 it was accompanied by a budget *deficit* of over 5 per cent of GDP and rising, which made monetary restraint technically and politically difficult, today there is a budget *surplus* of 3 per cent of GDP, of which privatisation contributes only one-third. Apart from obvious embarrassments of timing, the Government could today technically buy up the whole of the money supply with one

Figure 1: Return on Capital: Net Operating Surplus as a Percentage of Net Capital Stock

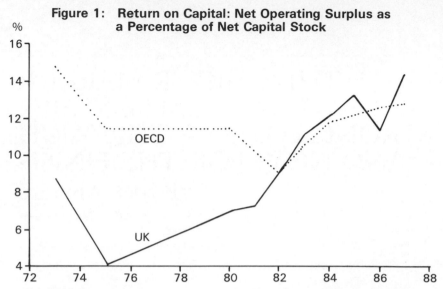

The OECD figures are an average of the USA, West Germany, France and Canada.

Source: As for footnote 1 (below).

year's surplus! Nor should past success in curbing money and inflation be forgotten: from 1982 to 1987 inflation, 13 per cent in 1979 and rising, was brought down to an average of under 5 per cent and money supply growth to 5·1 per cent.

If we turn from money to measures of productive performance, intimately related to labour market behaviour, the story is also one of sharp improvement. Productivity languished from 1973 to 1979, the last complete business cycle, with annual growth in both manufacturing and the whole economy of less than 1 per cent. Since 1979, it has been running at 4·5 per cent in manufacturing, and 3 per cent in the whole economy if one corrects for some recent measurement difficulties to do with part-timers and substitution within labour to cheaper types. These productivity growth rates over the last decade exceed all previous records for the British economy and also the 1980s performance of all other OECD countries apart from Japan.

With this turnround has come a surge in profitability. The rate of return on capital in British industry, according to a careful assessment by the Bank of England using OECD figures,[1] has risen from 6 per cent

---

[1] 'Rate of Return in Industry in UK and OECD', *Bank of England Quarterly Bulletin*, August 1988, p. 381.

in 1979—among the lowest in the OECD—to 14 per cent by 1987, among the highest (Figure 1).

Because unemployment has risen, the improvement in the growth of jobs since 1979 has not matched that in growth of productivity. Annual growth has averaged 2 per cent against 1·4 per cent from 1973 to 1979. But that includes the serious recession of 1980-81, as inflation was dramatically reduced. Since 1983, growth has run at more than 3 per cent every year. Unemployment is now falling rapidly and is only 0·5 million (about 1·5 per cent) above where it was in 1979.

Massive Overmanning

That may seem like failure. But here one has to step behind the figures to analyse the nature of unemployment in 1979. Because of massive overmanning, now widely conceded as a fact by industrialists in both the public and private sectors at that time, the unemployment was understated in the sense that it was only a matter of time before the overmanning too was moved onto the register. Mrs Thatcher's Government allowed this to happen without any attempt to subsidise or arm-twist industry to retain jobs.

So, as Figure 2 shows, true or underlying unemployment was already some 3 million by 1979 (the detailed basis for this calculation is given in Matthews and Minford, 1988). The next few years brought it out into the open and with it the deplorable uncompetitiveness of British industry. Had nothing else been done to restore profitability and efficiency, the labour shake-out would have been accompanied by a permanent loss of unprofitable output of a similar percentage. Productivity would not have improved and the economy would have contracted—never to recover.

Judged from this perspective, the fall in unemployment since 1986 represents a fall in largely inherited unemployment. It appears to be a genuine enough improvement, in that today few workers fear for the viability of their jobs—a far cry from the fragile job market of 1979.

To sum up the productive side, we have seen a dramatic improvement in the growth of productivity and profitability and a less dramatic improvement in economic growth itself as unemployment has risen. But that unemployment profile itself represents an underlying improvement because of the inheritance of overmanning in 1979. The facile Rip van Winkle comparisons conceal large changes in the underlying realities.

Figure 2: Unemployment, Actual and Equilibrium

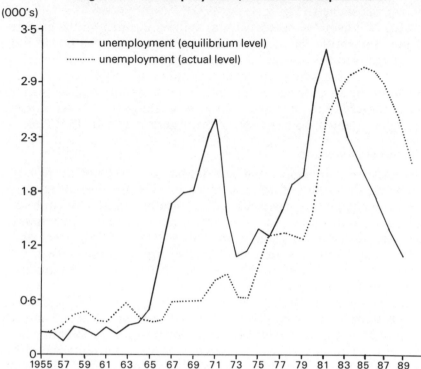

The Progress of Labour Market Reform

Virtually the whole gamut of supply-side reforms undertaken by the Thatcher governments have had impacts on the labour market, including privatisation, deregulation and contracting-out. But I want to focus here more narrowly on those policies which directly affected the motivation and organisation of labour.

First, there have been tax cuts, affecting incentives. Tax cuts have validated Mr Gladstone's experience: revenues from top taxpayers rose as their rates fell from 83 to 60 per cent, and in the economy generally average tax revenue has risen by about 4 per cent of GDP since 1979, even though marginal tax rates have generally been cut.

Union reform—namely, the cutback of union immunities from strike damages in a series of laws—has permitted managers to push through productivity deals accepted by workers but resisted by local and national union bosses. Working practices have changed sharply, as recently documented in research by labour economists at the London School of Economics (Wadwhani, 1989).

Finally, on the unemployment side there has been a steady stream of measures, which gathered pace from 1986 onwards, to loosen up the labour market and increase the incentives for workers to change jobs, retrain, and take lower-paid jobs in their own area. The welfare state support of the unemployed, combined with strong union powers over the wages of their protected members, were the major obstacles here. Curbing of, and more vigorous screening of eligibility for, unemployment benefits (the 'Restart' programme) and the union laws again have been the main means to roll back these obstacles. It was a pity that the crucial Restart programme was not initiated until July 1986, three long years after unemployment had passed 3 million. Nevertheless, as soon as it was introduced unemployment started to fall and has not yet stopped falling. Other relevant programmes have been the liberalisation of the rented housing market, cuts in taxes, and the reform of local authority taxation, important for regional regeneration.

So much is history. What went wrong was partly misdiagnosis— analysis in the early 1980s was still highly Keynesian as far as the labour market went and those who were pointing a different way were not sufficiently believed. Partly it was political: the difficulties of implementing tough policies towards benefits, the core of the problem, were obvious enough at the time, though after the success of Restart it is more difficult to remember just how daunting they appeared.

But once Lord Young had launched the Restart programme, the progress on unemployment was able to begin, and the many other policies which could contribute to that progress, such as the weakening of union power, lower tax rates, reformed in-work benefits, were able to come into their own on the unemployment front.

Today we are able to look at a labour market where unemployment is, at 5·8 per cent, lower than in most of Europe, less than half the rate of 1986, and, judging by recent trends as well as the evidence of the Liverpool model, heading towards 1 million by 1992.

What is the nature of that labour market today and what is needed to ensure this progress in the face of possible recession or other shocks?

The Evolving Labour Market

Not only is the unionised sector of the British economy getting steadily smaller, with union density down from a peak of 58 per cent in 1980 to

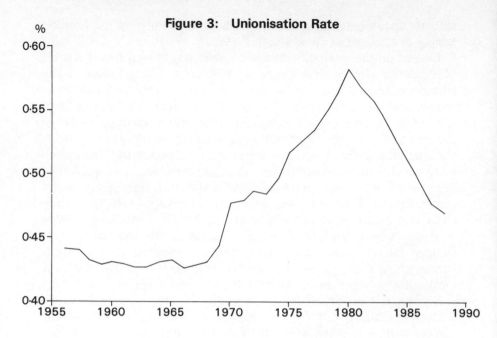

Figure 3: Unionisation Rate

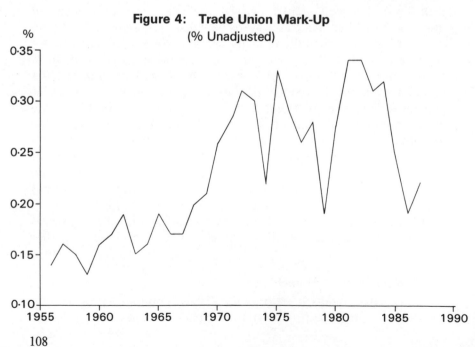

Figure 4: Trade Union Mark-Up
(% Unadjusted)

under 50 per cent in 1988 (Figure 3); but also, if we leave on one side the public sector, the nature of the unionised sector is changing.

There is a rising percentage of single union, no-strike deals. Longer-term contracts with price escalator clauses are more common. As illustrated in Figure 4, the mark-up of union pay over non-union pay has fallen, from a peak of 32 per cent, again in 1980, to 22 per cent by 1987; while this mark-up measure (estimated by the Centre for Labour Economics at the LSE from the New Earnings Surveys) is not highly refined it is generally considered a good indicator of the direction of the true mark-up over time.

It would also seem that individual contracts are becoming more meaningful. Even where a union bargains for workers, there is more widespread appraisal which affects the individual pay of workers within the general framework; and there is also more performance-linked pay. Workers are being more flexibly deployed: demarcation is breaking down (Daniel, 1987).

These trends are true of those in traditional full-time employment. However, additionally there has been a marked trend towards flexible employment: part-time, self-employment, and temporary contract work. This contributed 35 per cent of employment in 1986 as against 30 per cent in 1981 (Hakim, 1987).

The greater flexibility of wages that this would suggest is evidenced by the rise in the pay of skilled workers relative to unskilled, by no less than 20 per cent since 1979 (Figure 5). We know that particularly scarce skills, such as those of top managers, have seen much higher relative growth.

Declining union power in the traditional sense and the rise of pragmatic unionism linked to the aspirations of workers, who now have real union votes, have therefore meant that pay is now closely linked to productivity. Strong traditional unions, often helped by government incomes policies, were able to force employers to pay above productivity for certain—usually unskilled—categories of worker and below it for others. Unions of this type saw themselves as part of a redistributive socialist movement. The result was poor productivity and rising unemployment, as employers sought to reduce the ranks of unwanted unskilled workers and were unable to find scarce skilled workers to man productive operations.

Wage Demands to Be Curbed by Monetary Squeeze?

Clearly, we have had a period of uncomfortably high money supply growth and inflation. This has fuelled wage demands which are

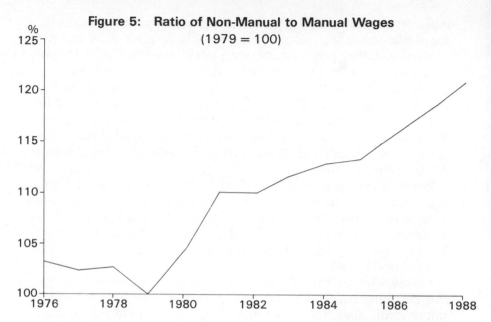

Figure 5: Ratio of Non-Manual to Manual Wages
(1979 = 100)

excessive relative to the current monetary environment. But money supply growth having been drastically curbed by the high interest rates of 1989, it is likely that wages too will before long be moderated.

Furthermore, we must not lose sight of this increased flexibility. We have every reason to believe that the growth of productivity is much faster today than it was in the 1970s, or even the 1960s. The CBI recently reported[2] that manufacturing productivity (among CBI members with current pay settlements) has been growing at 6·5 per cent in the past year, and is expected to continue to grow at 5 per cent in the coming year.

Although services productivity is poorly measured, the competition in the financial and other service sectors is now intense, and the new information technology can make enormous productivity gains; as in newspapers, it will require a major player to break the old mould of over-manned high street banks, for example, and the rest will then be forced to follow suit. It is arguable that the computer has even more potential in service industries than in manufacturing. With the advent of satellite broadcasting and new competition generally on the airwaves (Beesley and Laidlaw, 1989), wholesale changes in the service industries will follow.

---

[2] *CBI Pay Data Bank Survey*, 4th Quarter 1989.

Estimation of productivity trends is hazardous in the present murky state of our statistics, but a range of 3-4 per cent growth across the whole economy is quite plausible in these circumstances. That implies that 8-9 per cent wage rises are compatible with 5 per cent inflation.

The very fact that at present we have falling unemployment allied to real wage rises of over 4 per cent (wages at 9 per cent less wholesale prices at under 5 per cent) suggests that industrial productivity is growing faster than this. Real wages in services are growing more slowly, by around 3 per cent (9 per cent less service inflation of about 6 per cent); yet again employment here is growing fast so that productivity is likely to be exceeding this growth rate.

What Still Requires to Be Done?

There are two main areas where reform has further to go: the tax/ benefit system and union powers under the law.

Taxes and Benefits

High marginal tax rates still restrict individual incentives. If all taxes and benefits are included, the marginal tax rate on the average worker is still 45 per cent; this is the wedge between what the employer pays out and what the worker can buy in the shops. The marginal tax rate on the high-earning worker is 50 per cent. On the lowest-earning worker it ranges approximately from 75 to 95 per cent for the vast majority, reflecting the rate of benefit withdrawal for those on Family Credit and housing benefit.

There are those who believe that by rejigging the tax burden in subtle ways (e.g., switching from an income to an expenditure tax), incentives to work can be raised. This is not so: what matters is the wedge, and it matters not a jot who pays what part of this wedge. Since workers in a flexible labour market, such as we now have, are paid according to their productivity, and in a competitive goods market there is a going level of productivity that must be matched, the wedge, whoever pays it, has to be passed back to the worker; the employer effectively cannot afford to pay any more than the going rate of productivity. So incentives are affected one-for-one by all marginal tax rates.

Forty-five to 50 per cent is obviously too high a marginal tax rate. Paul Ashton and I (1989) have recently estimated the responses of work effort to incentives by a large sample of British men (over 7,000 in the 1980 General Household Survey). We found that for the average man the elasticity was 0·14, for higher earners it was 0·5, and for lower earners it was similarly high. This implies that a cut of 5 pence in the standard rate would raise work and output across the whole economy by a far from negligible 1 per cent. A similar cut in the top marginal rate would raise top earners' work and output by 4 per cent; this is of great significance given their high productivity.

As for the lower earners, it would appear that to cut their rates from the extraordinarily high 75-95 per cent (the 'poverty trap') must be a high priority. This of course is true. But unfortunately one way of doing it, that is, lowering the benefit withdrawal rate and so increasing benefits for those above the current benefit cut-off points, would incur a large fiscal cost. This would mean higher tax rates for the average worker, whose incentives would correspondingly be diminished. Since there are millions of them and only about half-a-million people in the poverty trap, the overall effect on work and output is negative (some detailed calculations are given in my paper on the poverty trap, 1990).

So this route is not promising: it would, so to speak, throw out the baby with the bathwater. Another route is less expensive but politically difficult. This is to reduce the benefit entitlements, so that there is less to withdraw, and thus a lower withdrawal rate for those in the poverty trap.

If this is ruled out on political grounds, one is left with a gradualist compromise. This is to maintain the benefit entitlements in absolute terms, that is to say, indexed to prices. But not to raise them as real wages rise. This policy would correspond to one of protecting people from absolute rather than 'relative' poverty.

Under this strategy, the poverty trap would be steadily alleviated by the general enrichment of the economy taking people out of it. As fewer and fewer people fell into the trap, it would be possible also to lower the withdrawal rate without excessive cost. With a reasonable growth rate of real wages and continued cuts in the standard rate of income tax, it would be possible to eliminate the poverty trap over a decade or so.

Union Power

The other main area is union power. (An empirical account of its effects can be found in Beenstock and Minford, 1988; more recently, Blanchflower and Oswald, 1989, have uncovered evidence in a large industrial sample of how unions have held back employment and output growth in unionised parts of British industry.) The closed shop

Figure 6: Industrial Disputes: Days Lost
(Per Thousand Employees in Employment)

will shortly have been abolished, and with surprisingly little protest. The immunities have been cut back, so that now only strikes about the strikers' own wages and conditions when supported by a ballot attract immunity; unofficial strikes will effectively be covered by this too when the new law goes through.

But the changes in the unionised sector discussed above have meant a much lower recourse to strikes and to closed shop provisions. The pre-entry closed shop has dwindled to near insignificance before the legislation which will finally kill it off. Days lost in strikes are now running at one-quarter of the average of the 1970s (Figure 6). It is as if union leaders and workers now accept that competitive practices must rule. Partly this reflects the greater competition in product markets, especially in recently deregulated and privatised or contracted-out industries. But partly too it reflects the real wage gains that have followed the rise in productivity made possible by the legislation: better working practices have massively benefited employees.

In short, it has begun to be realised that co-operation in labour relations pays off in rewards and avoids the penalties of being cut out by the product competition.

113

If co-operation is the name of the new labour game, then strike methods of settling disputes are wasteful. Just as courts of law are there to avoid fisticuffs, vendettas and duels between individuals and families, so agreed processes and arbitration are there to avoid expensive fights between workers and their managers.

If the matter is put this way, it is hard to see what role is left for immunities, which place one group, the union, above the common law of contract and tort. What sense can be assigned, in a law of due process, to one party being bound by no contract? (A question also put and answered negatively by Charles Hanson and Graham Mather, 1988.)

Immunities therefore seem quite out of date in this modern setting. Remember that immunities permit an outside party, namely a union, to induce its members to breach commercial contracts of employment. If immunities were withdrawn, it would still be possible for a union to call a strike without risking damages if a strike under certain circumstances was an agreed option under a commercial contract with the employer. But clearly it would require the signing of a collective contract, to bring the strike action within the law.

Whether, in the absence of immunities, unions and employers would sign collective contracts is a matter of conjecture; presumably they would, thus bringing an area of lawlessness within the ambit of the law. The whole business of strikes might well then recede into the background, in the face of a demand for less wasteful methods of settling differences. In Japanese businesses, for example, there is typically a no-strike agreement but provision for continuous consultation with workers' representatives as well as individual worker circles, and arbitration (often 'pendulum') as a final option. The Japanese have led the way in fruitful mass industrial relations.

Government has since 1906 interfered in and overridden the common law, with the best of 'social' intentions. Whatever the rights and wrongs of this history, the present situation seems to call for a restoration of the common law in this area. Private individuals, firms, unions and other groups of worker representatives can then work out their own voluntary arrangements for relating to one another within the law, as the policeman of their voluntary contracts.

Such a total abolition of immunities would complete the step-by-step process of law reform in industrial relations, which was begun in 1980. Now that we can see more clearly to what sort of industrial relations world the previous reforms have led all the parties, in a way that has been generally welcomed, it is possible for us to see that this final step would be no piece of brutal union-bashing but rather a logical creation of a legal framework within which worker rights could be voluntarily defined and impartially protected. Industrial relations would then finally be on a solid, simple and harmonious basis.

I have left on one side the question of public sector unions. Here there is old-fashioned product monopoly and producer monopsony of labour. The public sector monopoly unions still face the government monopsonist across the bargaining table in time-honoured fashion.

If public monopolies are privatised and broken up or otherwise exposed to effective competition, then they can be assimilated into the private sector as already discussed. But suppose there is a rump left with which nothing can be done. Do they constitute an exception to our previous analysis and proposed solution?

I cannot see that they do. Without immunities even these neanderthal opponents will have a strong incentive to regulate their agreements under the law. If they do not, both will lose from the resulting breakdown of industrial co-operation; even in the absence of a collective agreement, the union is able legally to organise its members to withdraw from their previous contracts. No doubt the upshot will be what is found in a number of other public sectors: the routine use of pendulum arbitration.

Conclusion

We have seen in the UK a remarkable change in the behaviour of the labour market and the climate of industrial relations. Co-operation is now the rule inside firms, as indeed it ought to be in any properly functioning productive unit. To carry forward this process, we must once more allow the law full sway over free voluntary contracts. This argues for the abolition of the immunities which override the law and which prevent the interplay of normal commercial contracting in this crucial area.

Marginal tax rates are also still too high to permit private individuals to achieve their full potential. Both standard and top rates should be cut. The poverty trap is a serious problem for a small group; it should be gradually eliminated by pegging benefits in real terms and allowing real wage growth and tax cuts to reduce numbers in the trap to insignificance. As the numbers fall, the withdrawal rates in the trap can also be steadily cut.

Finally, all this assumes that other reforms are consolidated.

115

'Restart' and the curbing of benefit fraud must continue to be tough, as always intended in the Beveridge founding plans. The rented housing market must be freed to help mobility away from unemployment black spots. Labour regulations (on hiring and firing, for instance), loosened impressively over the last decade, must be kept under review: the UK's regulatory system is considered by industry the least burdensome in Europe (Emerson, 1988)—and it must stay that way, at the least. Wage councils in particular should be phased out completely.

The discussions of the EEC Commission's Social Charter have raised a question mark over the progress achieved in these areas. However, considerable obscurity surrounds both these ideas and the legality under the EEC treaties of their imposition on unwilling member-states. With so much in flux in Europe at present after the liberation of its Eastern part, it seems unlikely that the EEC will wish to become embroiled in controversy over such marginal matters. Certainly aspects of the Charter as expounded by certain Commissioners would be out of the question in the UK, since they would reverse the remarkable progress achieved over the past decade, let alone imperil the further progress discussed here.

REFERENCES

Beenstock, M. and P. Minford (1987): 'Curing Unemployment through Labour-Market Competition', in P. Minford (ed.), *Monetarism and Macro-economics*, IEA Readings No. 26, London: Institute of Economic Affairs, pp. 129-49.

Beesley, M. and B. Laidlaw (1989): *The Future of Telecommunications*, Research Monograph 42, London: Institute of Economic Affairs.

Blanchflower, D. and A. Oswald (1988): 'The Economic Effect of British Trade Unions', Discussion Paper No. 324, Centre for Labour Economics, London School of Economics.

Daniel, W. (1987): *Workplace Industrial Relations and Technical Change*, London: Pinter Publishers.

Emerson, M. (1988): 'Regulation or deregulation of the labour market: policy regimes for the recruitment and dismissal of employees in the industrialised countries', *European Economic Review*, Vol. 32, No. 4, Amsterdam: Elsevier Science Publications, pp. 775-817.

Hakim, C. (1987): 'Trends in the flexible workforce', *Employment Gazette*, Department of Employment, November issue, pp. 549-58.

Hanson, C. and G. Mather (1988): *Striking out Strikes*, Hobart Paper No. 110, London: Institute of Economic Affairs.

Matthews, K. and P. Minford (1987): 'Mrs. Thatcher's economic policies 1979-87', *Economic Policy*, October 1987, pp. 57-101.

Minford, P. (1990): 'The poverty trap after the Fowler reforms', in W. Eltis and K. Mayhew (eds.), Proceedings of NEDO Conference on Incentives for the Poor (forthcoming).

Minford, P. and P. Ashton (1989): 'The poverty trap and the Laffer curve: what can the GHS tell us?', CEPR working paper, revised December 1989, Liverpool (mimeo).

Wadwhani, S. (1989): 'The effects of unions on productivity growth, investment and employment—a report on some recent work', Discussion Paper No. 356, Centre for Labour Economics, London School of Economics, August.

9

THE KEYS TO SUCCESS: CONSUMING LESS AND PRODUCING MORE

Bill Robinson

Director, Institute for Fiscal Studies

What Went Wrong?

I SHALL BEGIN by stating that something has gone wrong. In a nutshell it is that domestic demand has been allowed to grow too fast for too long. The rate of growth of demand since 1987 has clearly exceeded the rate of growth of supply. The immediate consequence has been a current account deficit of alarming proportions. The longer-term worry is that that deficit, which I interpret as suppressed inflation, gradually turns into overt inflation. That process is already under way— the GDP deflator has accelerated from under 3 per cent in 1986 to over 8 per cent in the first half of 1989.

It is hard to see a rapid improvement in 1990, since wage growth is over 9 per cent, and output growth is unlikely to be more than 2 per cent, and could well be less. If unit costs grow by 7 per cent or more, it is unlikely that inflation will fall below this level.

What has caused demand to run out of control? The popular view is that Mr Lawson perpetrated a series of disastrous policy errors in 1988. He cut taxes by £4 billion. He cut interest rates to 8 per cent in a vain attempt to shadow the deutschemark. And to cap it all, he announced at Budget time that mortgage interest relief would be limited to £30,000 of borrowing per dwelling rather than per person with effect

TABLE 1

CONSUMER SPENDING: FORECASTS AND OUTTURNS,
1987 AND 1988
(*annual percentage changes*)

Forecasts	1987	1988
National Institute[1]	4·3	2·9
London Business School[1]	3·9	3·3
HM Treasury[2]	4	4
Outturn	5·4	6·9

[1] Forecast for year made in February of that year.
[2] Budget forecast published in March.

from 1 August. The incentive to borrow, in the limited period while rates were low and the tax concession remained in place, was enormous. The resulting borrowing binge, and the associated house price boom, is now history.

With hindsight we can all see that there were policy mistakes. Yet I certainly do not believe that errors of judgement in the 1988 Budget were mainly, let alone solely, responsible for our present plight. As Table 1 shows, for two years in a row the three main macro-economic models underestimated the growth of consumer spending in their beginning of year forecasts—a palpable miss in 1987 and by a mile in 1988. What was going on that the models failed to spot? I believe there were two important changes to the economic environment that took us into uncharted territory: the de-regulation of financial markets, and the record fall in unemployment.

I assume that everybody has by now been told a hundred times that consumer spending has grown faster than expected because of the astonishing collapse of the personal savings ratio. A point that has not been so frequently made is that the behaviour of savings in the current boom has been quite different from its behaviour in past booms. Table 2 shows the growth of consumer spending, and decomposes it into the part that can be explained by the growth of real personal disposable income, and the residual, which reflects the change in the savings ratio. It shows clearly how, in both the Heath-Barber and the Healey booms, real incomes were allowed to race ahead, by an astonishing 15 per cent in 1972-73 and by nearly 13 per cent in 1978-79. On both occasions consumers chose not to spend all this largesse, and savings rose.

TABLE 2

INCOME, SAVING AND SPENDING IN THREE CYCLES

A. THE PRESENT CYCLE

	Changes in real incomes	+	Change in saving ratio (+ means fall)	=	Change in real spending
1986	3·7		1·9		5·6
1987	3·6		1·8		5·4
1988	4·9		2·0		6·9
1989	3·3		0·4		3·7
1990	3		−2		1

B. EARLIER CYCLES

(i) Heath-Barber Boom & OPEC I

	Income	Saving	Spending
1972	8·4	−2·3	6·1
1973	6·4	−1·2	5·2
1974	−0·8	−0·7	−1·5
1975	0·5	−1·1	−0·6
1976	−0·1	+0·4	0·3

(ii) Healey Boom & OPEC II

	Income	Saving	Spending
1978	7·2	−1·7	5·5
1979	5·6	−1·4	4·2
1980	1·5	−1·5	−1·0
1981	−1·3	1·5	0·2
1982	−0·1	0·7	0·8

The latest boom looks quite different. Real personal disposable income has accelerated slowly since the economy emerged from recession in 1982, averaging 2¼ per cent in 1983-85. As Table 2 shows, it has run at around 3½ per cent in 1986-89, apart from the 5 per cent growth recorded in 1988.

Figure 1:   Main Causes of the Consumer Boom

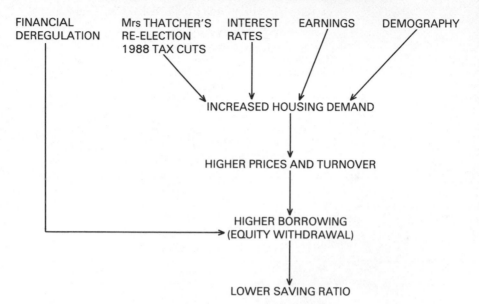

Taking these figures together, I would argue that real incomes have not been allowed to grow any faster than the growth of productive potential over the decade as a whole; that the acceleration of income growth from 1986 onwards was not disastrous since it was matched by some acceleration of potential growth and there was in any case still some spare capacity; and that the 5 per cent growth in incomes in 1988 supports the view that Mr Lawson went over the top in that year.

Consumption Outstrips Real Income Growth

But, and this is the key point, I am prepared to assert that we would not be in our present difficulties if the growth of consumption had merely matched the growth of real incomes in the 1980s. Our troubles have occurred because consumer spending has grown consistently faster than income, especially since 1986, in a way that we have never before witnessed in an economic upswing.

Why did that happen? There is no single explanation—as is usually the case in economics when extraordinary events occur. Figure 1 illustrates, informally, the main causes of the consumer boom. The expected income growth of the better-off was increased by the re-election of Mrs Thatcher in 1987 and the tax cuts in 1988. Financial

TABLE 3
NUMBER OF YOUNG PEOPLE
(*thousands*)

Age Group	1979	1988
20 – 24	4,053	4,739
25 – 29	3,874	4,501
20 – 29	7,927	9,246

de-regulation made it easy for them to borrow against these enhanced income expectations, and the fall in interest rates encouraged them to do so.

That is all standard stuff. I would add to that story, drawing on insights gleaned from the IFS/LBS micro-to-macro research programme, that the housing market played a crucial role as a channel for the extra borrowing. Much of the borrowing was for house purchase. A demographic bulge of young people buying their first house underpinned the market, generating a rise in turnover which gave many people the opportunity to withdraw from the market some of the equity generated by the rise in house prices. Table 3 shows that the number of 20-29 year-olds increased by nearly 1·5 million between 1979 and 1988.

Figure 2 shows that the number of home-owners with a mortgage in that age group increased by even more. The 'yuppie' phenomenon is clearly visible in the statistics. Figure 2 is constructed by multiplying the population statistics by the proportion of home-owners with a mortgage, as revealed by the Family Expenditure Survey. The long upward trend in owner-occupation was halted by the 1980 recession, but accelerated from 1983 onwards as confidence recovered and interest rates came down.

It is not surprising that this sharp increase in demand for housing should have contributed to a major house price boom. The house-price-to-income ratio rose to a cyclical peak comparable with that attained in the infamous Heath-Barber boom. Since housing accounts for half of personal wealth, it is also unsurprising that house-owners should have been encouraged by their increased wealth to step up their spending. What does require an explanation, however, is that spending should have risen so much more (relative to income) in 1987-88 than it

**Figure 2: Number of Owner-Occupiers With Mortgage
Aged 20-29**

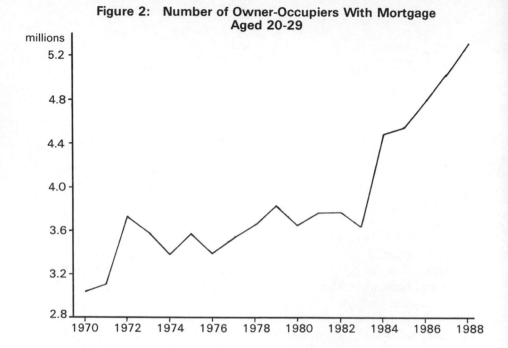

did in 1972-73. The answer must surely be that financial liberalisation
has made it much easier to borrow. The wealth effect on consumption
is thus now much greater than before. The econometric models
have only just begun to take account of this change. That is the main
reason why they so dramatically failed to predict consumer spending
in 1987-88.

Effect of Rise in Employment on Savings and Incomes

But before I leave the subject of what went wrong I would like to draw
attention to another aspect of the boom that has received less attention
than it deserves. The acceleration of income that we noted in 1986
coincided with the (long-awaited) downturn in unemployment.
Although employment had started to rise in 1983, most of the new jobs
created went to part-time women. The labour market for prime-age
males did not start to tighten significantly until 1987, when
unemployment began to fall. The increase in employment in 1988, at
nearly 3 per cent, was the largest annual increase on record, well above
the increase recorded in 1973.

TABLE 4

THE GROWTH OF REAL INCOME IN 1988

		Per cent
1.	Wages per head	8·0
2.	Consumer price	5·0
3.	Real income per head (1 – 2)	3·0
4.	Employment	2·8
5.	Tax cuts	0·8
6.	Growth of real income (3 + 4 + 5)	6·6
7.	Actual growth	4·9

There are two possible consequences of this rise in employment. It may have contributed to the unexpected fall in the savings ratio. The precautionary motive for saving is certainly lower when unemployment is falling, since the chance of losing your job, and hence the importance of saving for a rainy day, is reduced. Certainly many American economists believe in this relationship, for which econometric evidence can be found in US data. It is harder to find such a relationship in the UK data, but it may nevertheless be there.

However, it is the effect of the rise in employment on incomes that I wish to explore. Obviously the return to work of all these people must have boosted incomes. Table 4 presents some crude calculations. In 1988 wages per head grew by 8·0 per cent and consumer prices by 5·0 per cent, so real incomes per head grew by 3·0 per cent. If we add in growth of employment at 2·8 per cent, and three-quarters of the £4·2 billion of tax cuts, which added a further 0.8 per cent to disposable income in the calendar year 1988, we arrive at an estimated growth of real income of 6·6 per cent. Of course this is an overestimate, because those newly employed were not previously receiving nothing. Nevertheless, it is surprising that the growth of real personal disposable income is officially estimated at only 4·9 per cent in 1988.

These considerations suggest that the rise in income may have been larger than officially estimated. This would be consistent with the evidence from the official output data. The fall in the savings ratio is a statistical deduction, based on independent estimates of income and spending. Like all balances which are the difference between two large numbers, it is subject to considerable margins of error. Despite the fall in saving, there has been little change in the rate at which the personal sector has continued to acquire financial assets. The measured rise in borrowing does not match the apparent fall in saving.

If incomes have been underestimated, then there is less of a puzzle over savings behaviour, particularly in 1988. But it is highly unlikely that the puzzle can be made to disappear altogether. So I stand by my conclusion that what has mainly gone wrong has been an unexpected surge in spending relative to income. But it also seems possible that policy-makers have in recent years been steering the economy with a faulty compass. As in 1972-73, the economy has been allowed to grow too fast partly because the statistics have not revealed just how fast it has been growing.

How to Put Matters Right

Once diagnosis has been made it is easy to prescribe the cure. If our problems have been caused by the collapse of savings, presumably the solution lies in a revival of savings. All we have to do is spend less than we earn for a year or two, to correct the imbalances caused by spending more than we earned in 1987-89. The balance-of-payments problem reflects a shortage of national savings (which is the sum of the savings of persons, companies and the government) relative to national investment. We can cure the problem by cutting investment and/or by boosting the savings of any one of these economic agents.

A cutback in investment is clearly undesirable, since the long-term solution to our problem is to boost output relative to demand. So we should be looking for ways to increase savings. Since it is the savings of the personal sector that have collapsed, it is tempting to argue that the cure must lie in boosting personal savings.

The obvious solution, given the links between the collapse of the savings ratio and the rise in borrowing, is to rein back borrowing. There are two possibilities: to make borrowing more expensive; or to impose credit controls. Given that the problems have been caused by financial liberalisation, it is tempting to argue that the solution lies in reversing that process. However, the fact is that liberalisation is irreversible. The main effect of trying to restrict borrowing would be to drive the business off-shore. The damage to London as a financial centre would be immense.

The alternative, to raise interest rates, has been in place since May 1988. The policy has undesirable side-effects—the DTI investment intentions survey shows a rise in volume next year of only 1 per cent, following a three-year period in which real investment growth has averaged 16 per cent. But it is undoubtedly working. The housing boom has come to an end. Consumer confidence is at its lowest level since 1982. Retailers have avoided a miserable Christmas only by savage discounting. It appears that the fall in the savings ratio has been halted.

Does anything else need to be done? I believe so. My worry is that real incomes are still growing at some 2-3 per cent. If the slowdown in consumer spending improves the current account, as sooner or later it must, a revival of foreign confidence could reverse international capital movements and present the Government with a new policy dilemma: cut interest rates or face a sharp appreciation of the pound. If interest rates are cut, consumer spending might too quickly revive, plunging us back into our present difficulties. If, on the other hand, interest rates remain high, the resulting rise in sterling may choke off the encouraging revival of exports.

The solution under these circumstances is surely to rein back consumer spending by damping down the expectations of growing incomes on which borrowing is based. A good start would be to indicate that the 20 per cent tax rate promise—like the zero inflation target—remains in place but only as a long-term goal (i.e., in practice the Government will settle for a 25 per cent tax rate just as it has always settled for 5 per cent inflation). This signal should be given in the 1990 Budget—the first Budget of a new Chancellor is the perfect moment for a strategic change of this sort. And words should be backed by actions—that is, a tight Budget—to show that any expectation of fiscal largesse to come is misplaced.

To sum up, I believe that what has gone wrong has been mainly an unexpected surge in borrowing, though it is also possible that incomes have been underestimated. I believe that the high interest-rate policy is bringing the situation back under control. But to keep the economy on course in 1990, and to give the Government some freedom of manoeuvre on interest rates (which it may need to steer sterling into the EMS), the fiscal stance should be tightened in the 1990 Budget.

The UK in the World 'Tax Market'

The suggestion that the Government should now stop cutting taxes leads me neatly to the third topic I have been asked to address. Where has a decade of (sporadic) tax reform left the UK tax system, and how

127

TABLE 5

UK TAXES, SPENDING AND BORROWING
UNDER MRS THATCHER

% of GDP	Tax receipts	+	Borrowing	=	Spending
1979/80	38½		5		43½
1989/90	40¾		–2½		38¾

Source: *Autumn Statement* and *Financial Statistics*.

TABLE 6

TAXES AS A SHARE OF GDP:
SELECTED COUNTRIES, 1979 AND 1987

	1979	1987
UK	38·3	40·7
EC	41·5	45·4
USA	30·5	32·0
JAPAN	26·3	33·2
OECD	34·9	37·2

do we compare with other countries? In answering the question we should examine both average and marginal tax rates.

Looking first at average tax rates, which measure the overall burden of taxation, we find that they have changed remarkably little over the Thatcher decade. But, on reflection, this should not surprise us. As Table 5 shows, government spending is financed by a combination of taxes and borrowing. The Government has achieved a significant reduction in spending as a share of GDP. But that has been matched by the fall in borrowing, rather than by a reduction in the overall tax burden. The much-trumpeted reduction in the basic rate of income tax was paid for in the early days by an increase in the VAT rate and by oil taxes; over the period as a whole, however, the most important offset has been steadily rising National Insurance contributions and latterly the buoyancy of corporation tax.

Holding the tax burden constant is in itself quite an unusual achievement. The natural buoyancy of tax revenue in most tax systems, which have a built-in progressivity, plus the high income

TABLE 7

HOW THE TAX BURDEN WAS SPREAD IN 1987
(% of GDP)

	Personal income	Corporate income	Social Security	Consumption
UK	10	4	7	11
EC	11	3	12	12½
USA	11	2½	8½	4½
Japan	7	7	8½	3½
OECD	12	3	9½	11

Note: OECD and EC totals are unweighted averages.

elasticity of demand for many publicly provided goods, means that the share of tax in GDP has risen steadily over the years in the OECD. The 1980s, though billed as a decade of tax reform and tax reduction, has been no exception. Table 6 shows that the UK had an average tax rate slightly below the EC average and distinctly above the OECD average in 1980. By 1987 Britain had an average tax burden well below the EC average but still above that of the OECD.

The average tax burden in the OECD as a whole is lower than for the EC because the USA and Japan are more lightly taxed than European countries. The average tax burden in any country depends ultimately on the share of GDP devoted to public spending. This is much lower in the USA than in Europe because health is in the private rather than the public sector. It is much lower in Japan than in Europe because the Japanese spend virtually nothing on defence.

Table 7 shows how the higher European tax burden is borne. If we divide taxes into four main categories, it can be seen that the Japanese and Americans pay far less in indirect taxes (purchase tax, sales tax, VAT, specific duties, etc.) than we do in Europe. Table 7 also shows a higher corporate tax burden in Japan and, to a lesser extent, the UK. How does this square with the conventional image of the UK as a country whose corporate tax reform in 1984 put it firmly in the van of the tax-cutting movement of the 1980s?

There is no great mystery. Corporate tax receipts have risen as a share of GDP because corporate profits have been buoyant. The recovery of profits started well before the cut in taxes, and if I had to choose a single cause, it would be the removal of exchange controls,

TABLE 8

CORPORATE TAX RATES

	National Tax Rate	Type of Tax System	Local Taxes	Imputation Rate
Belgium	43	Imputation		33·3
Denmark	50	Imputation		20
France	42	Imputation		33·3
Germany	36/56	Split Rate/ Imputation	15	36
Greece	44	Imputation		44
Ireland	10	Imputation		5·3
Italy	36	Imputation	16·2	36
Luxembourg	36 + 0·72	Classical	6	—
Netherlands	35	Classical		—
Portugal	35/47	Split Rate		—
Spain	35	Imputation		9·1
UK	35	Imputation		25
Japan	32/42	Split Rate	12	—
USA	34	Classical	3·5	—

Source: OECD (1989), reproduced from IFS Report Series No. 35, p. 39. See original for qualifications.

which led ineluctably to a levelling up of the rate of return on UK investment towards the world level.

It is also true that other countries' corporation tax rates are not uniformly higher than our own, as Table 8 shows. But there is also an important point about average *versus* marginal tax rates which is worth drawing out. Many tax systems can be characterised, in simple algebra, by the formula shown in Table 9A. In such systems it is possible to lower the marginal rate of tax if allowances are simultaneously reduced. Table 9B shows an example tax from the personal income tax system. The clearest example of an allowance in the tax system is the personal allowance. But the concept goes much wider. Mortgage interest relief, relief for pensions contributions, the depreciation allowances that companies get on their investments—all these are examples of allowances which reduce the taxable base, and hence increase the marginal rate that is required to achieve a given revenue target.

TABLE 9

TAX REFORM: AVERAGE AND MARGINAL RATES

A. Some Simple Algebra

T	= t	(Y – A)
Tax revenue	= tax rates x (tax base – allowance)	
T/Y	= t	– A/Y
Average rate	= marginal rate – allowance/base	

Tax reform: lower marginal rate
and lower allowance
leave *average* rate unchanged

B. A Numerical Example

	£	£
Income	10,000	10,000
Allowance	6,000	2,000
Taxable income	4,000	8,000
Marginal tax rate	40%	20%
Tax bill	1,600	1,600
Average tax rate	*16%*	*16%*

We have only to enumerate these possibilities to see that the UK tax reforms of the 1980s have not been very radical. Life assurance premium relief has been abolished. Mortgage interest relief has been reduced in real terms. Initial investment allowances have been abolished. These changes have made some revenue available for rate reductions. But the headline-grabbing reductions in the basic and higher rates of income tax have mainly been paid for out of the reduction in public spending as a share of GDP and the natural buoyancy of the revenue.

Conclusion

I conclude that the tax changes of the 1980s, which were remarkable by past standards even if not by the standard of what, theoretically at least, still waits to be done, have left the UK with a fairly low average tax burden by European standards. We remain more highly taxed than the USA and Japan. And there is little evidence that we have been more successful than other countries in tilting our tax schedules so as to achieve particularly low marginal rates of tax. If we wish to save and produce our way out of our present difficulties, much remains to be done: higher *average* rates of tax to raise (public) savings; lower *marginal* rates to encourage production.

IEA PUBLICATIONS
Subscription Service

An annual subscription is the most convenient way to obtain our publications. Every title we produce in all our regular series will be sent to you immediately on publication and without further charge, representing a substantial saving.

Individual subscription rates*

Britain: £25·00 p.a. including postage.
£23·00 p.a. if paid by Banker's Order.
£15·00 p.a. to teachers and students who pay *personally.*

Europe: £25·00 p.a. including postage.

South America: £35·00 p.a. or equivalent.

Other Countries: Rates on application. In most countries subscriptions are handled by local agents. Addresses are available from the IEA.

* These rates are *not* available to companies or to institutions.

To: The Treasurer, Institute of Economic Affairs,
2 Lord North Street, Westminster,
London SW1P 3LB

I should like to subscribe from ....

I enclose a cheque/postal order for:

☐ £25·00

☐ £15·00   I am a teacher/student at ....

....

☐ Please send a Banker's Order form.

☐ Please send an invoice.

☐ Please charge my credit card:

Please tick   ☐ **VISA**   ☐ ▲   ☐ AMERICAN EXPRESS   ☐ ◑

Card No: ⬚⬚⬚⬚ ⬚⬚⬚⬚ ⬚⬚⬚⬚ ⬚⬚⬚⬚

In addition I would like to purchase the following previously published titles:

....

....

Name ....

Address ....

....

.... Post Code ....

⎫
⎬ BLOCK
⎭ LETTERS
PLEASE

Signed .... Date ....

RP31

THE AUTHORS

Bill Martin is Chief Economist (UK), UBS Phillips & Drew, responsible for its main monthly forecasts and for detailed commentary on the economy and on developments in government policy. He was educated at the University of Exeter where he obtained his first economics degree with honours and went on to an MSc at the University of Wales, Cardiff, where he specialised in international economics. He joined the Department of Trade and Industry as a member of the Government economic service in 1973 where he worked on a variety of aspects of the UK economy, briefing Ministers and contributing to the Treasury's macro-economic forecasts. He moved to the Cabinet office in 1981 and served as a member of the Central Policy Review Staff, better known as the 'Think Tank'. He was appointed Special Economic Adviser to the House of Commons Select Committee on the Treasury and Civil Service in 1985.

Giles Keating is Chief Economist and a Director, Research, of Credit Suisse First Boston. He holds a BA in Philosophy, Politics and Economics from St Catherine's College, Oxford, and an MSc in Mathematical Economics and Econometrics from the London School of Economics. He has published a number of articles on macro-economic issues in academic journals, most recently 'A Two-Good Model with Capital Accumulation and a Real Balance Effect', *Oxford Economic Papers* (1987), and 'Capital Asset Pricing under Alternative Policy Régimes', *Economic Modelling* (1988). He writes a regular column for *Nihon Keizai Shimbun* and for *The Times*. He is author of *The Production and Use of Economic Forecasts* (1985).

Walter Eltis is Director General, National Economic Development Office (NEDO). He was Economics Director (NEDO), from 1986-88, Fellow and Economics Tutor, Exeter College, Oxford, 1963-88. He is the author of *Classical Theory of Economic Growth* (1984); *Growth and Distribution* (1973); co-author with Robert Bacon of *Britain's Economic Problem: Too Few Producers* (1976); and he has published articles on

Adam Smith and François Quesnay. For the IEA he contributed (with Robert Bacon) 'How Growth in Public Expenditure has Contributed to Britain's Difficulties', in *The Dilemmas of Government Expenditure* (Readings No. 15, 1976); 'Public Policy', in *Job Creation—or Destruction?* (Readings No. 20, 1979); and 'The Need to Cut Public Expenditure and Taxation', in *Is Monetarism Enough?* (IEA Readings No. 24, 1980).

David Lomax is Group Economic Adviser, National Westminster Bank, and Editor of *National Westminster Bank Quarterly Review*. He was educated at Cambridge University and Stanford University, California. He is author (with P. T. Gutmann) of *The Euromarkets and International Financial Policies*; *The Developing Country Debt Crisis*; *London Markets After the Financial Services Act*. He is author of numerous articles and a regular broadcaster.

Jonathan Haskel was educated at the University of Bristol and the London School of Economics. From 1987-88 he was a lecturer in economics at Bristol. Since 1988 he has been at the Centre for Business Strategy, London Business School, and currently teaches Economics for Business on the LBS MBA programme. He is the author (with Richard Jackman) of 'Long Term Unemployment and the Effects of the Community Programme', *Oxford Bulletin of Economics and Statistics* (November 1988); (with Richard Jackman *et al.*) *A Job Guarantee for Long-Term Unemployed People*, Employment Institute (1989); (with Paul Geroski) 'Beyond the Hype—the Effects of 1992', Employment Institute *Economic Report* (September 1989).

John Kay, who was educated at the University of Edinburgh and Nuffield College, Oxford, is Professor of Industrial Policy and Director of the Centre for Business Strategy at the London Business School. He was previously the first Research Director of the Institute for Fiscal Studies, to which he was appointed in 1979, and became the Institute's Director in 1981. He is a Fellow of St John's College, Oxford. From 1971 to 1978 he was a lecturer in economics at the University of Oxford. He is the author or editor of several books, including (with Mervyn King) *The British Tax System* (1978); *The Reform of Social Security* (1984); (with Colin Mayer and David Thompson) (eds.) *Privatisation and Regulation—The UK Experience* (1986). For the IEA he contributed 'The Forms of Regulation', in *Financial Regulation—or Over-Regulation?* (IEA Readings No. 27, 1988).

Gordon Pepper is an Honorary Visiting Professor in the Department of Banking and Finance and Director of the Midland Montagu Centre for Financial Markets at the City University Business School. He is a member of the Economic and Social Research Council.

He is also a Director and Senior Adviser of Midland Montagu, which includes the stockbroking business of Greenwell Montagu. Gordon Pepper was previously Chairman of Greenwell Montagu & Co. and, prior to that, Joint Senior Partner of W. Greenwell & Co.

He was educated at Repton School and Trinity College, Cambridge, where he graduated in mathematics and economics.

In 1960 he was the joint founder of the gilt-edged business of W. Greenwell & Co. and revolutionised statistical techniques in the gilt-edged market and for many years was regarded as the leading commentator on the UK gilt-edged market. In 1972 he introduced W. Greenwell & Co.'s *Monetary Bulletin* which became one of the most widely read monetary economic publications produced in the United Kingdom.

He is a Fellow of the Institute of Actuaries and a Fellow of the Society of Investment Analysts.

Tim Congdon is Economic Adviser with Gerrard & National. He was educated at Colchester Royal Grammar School and St John's College and Nuffield College, Oxford. He was formerly an economics journalist with *The Times*; Senior Economist and Economics Partner, L. Messel; Chief Economist (UK), Shearson Lehman Hutton.

He is the author of *Monetary Control in Britain* (1982); *The Debt Threat* (1988); *Monetarism: an essay in definition* (1978); *Against Import Controls* (1981); *Economic Liberalism in the Cone of Latin America* (1985); and of a dictionary of economics. His latest publication is a pamphlet on recent British economic policy, *Monetarism Lost: and why it must be regained* (1989). Tim Congdon is one of the City of London's leading financial commentators, and a contributor to *The Times*, *Spectator*, and the IEA's *Economic Affairs*.

A. P. L. (Patrick) Minford has been Edward Gonner Professor of Applied Economics, University of Liverpool, since 1976. Formerly Visiting Hallsworth Research Fellow, University of Manchester,

135

1974-75. Sometime Consultant to the Ministry of Overseas Development, Ministry of Finance (Malawi), Courtaulds, Treasury, British Embassy (Washington). Editor of *National Institute Economic Review*, 1975-76. He is the author of *Substitution Effects, Speculation and Exchange Rate Stability* (1978), and of essays published in *Inflation in Open Economies* (1976); *The Effects of Exchange Adjustments* (1977); *On How to Cope with Britain's Trade Position* (1977); *Contemporary Economic Analysis* (1978); co-author of *Unemployment: Cause and Cure* (1983, 2nd edn. 1985).

Professor Minford is a Senior Research Fellow at the IEA and a member of the IEA's Advisory Council. He has contributed papers to *The Taming of Government* (IEA Readings No. 21, 1979); *Is Monetarism Enough?* (IEA Readings No. 24, 1980); *Could Do Better* (Occasional Paper 62, 1982); *The Unfinished Agenda* (1986); and *Reaganomics and After* (IEA Readings No. 28, 1989). He was joint author (with Michael Peel and Paul Ashton) of *The Housing Morass* (Hobart Paperback 25, IEA, 1987), and edited and introduced *Monetarism and Macro-economics* (IEA Readings No. 26, 1987).

Bill Robinson is Director of the Institute for Fiscal Studies, and has become an active participant in the debate on the British tax system. He was educated at St Edmund's Hall, Oxford, and did his postgraduate training at the University of Sussex and the London School of Economics. After a brief stint with IBM he worked as a professional economist in Whitehall (Cabinet Office and HM Treasury) and in Brussels (European Commission). He joined the London Business School in 1978 and was in charge of economic forecasting and editor of *Economic Outlook* from 1980-86. He has edited the latest three IFS 'Green Budget' publications and is a regular speaker and broadcaster both on macro-economic affairs and on taxation. He retains an interest in exchange rate policy and forecasting, and is still a regular contributor to the LBS *Exchange Rate Outlook*, which he edited from 1979-86. In Autumn 1988 he was invited to join the Retail Prices Advisory Committee as one of the independent experts who advise on the construction of the Retail Price Index.

Hobart Paperback 28

PRIVATISATION *&* COMPETITION

A Market Prospectus

Edited by Cento Veljanovski

Privatisation of the nationalised industries has been the hallmark of the Thatcher government's efforts to rejuvenate the British economy. Yet in key industries privatisation has not been accompanied by a coherent or consistent attempt to maximise competitive pressures. There is growing concern that in the utility industries – telecommunications, gas, electricity, water and transport – monopolies have been transferred to private ownership and regulation has replaced public ownership.

The fifteen contributors to *Privatisation & Competition* examine the interplay between privatisation, competition and regulation so far to identify the trade-offs, tensions and the probable consequences of the sacrifice of market forces and competitive pressures in Britain's privatisation programme. Many of the contributors put forward proposals for reform and blueprints for the privatisation of those industries which are still in the public sector – British Coal, the Electricity Supply Industry, British Rail and the Post Office.

Privatisation & Competition brings together an authoritative collection of original essays on one of the most radical and profound changes in industrial policy in Britain this century.

Contents

ISBN 0-255 36211-0   x + 242 pages   Royal Octavo   £9.50

INSTITUTE OF ECONOMIC AFFAIRS, 2 LORD NORTH STREET, WESTMINSTER, LONDON SW1P 3LB